Cambridge Elements ≡

Elements in Organization Theory
edited by
Nelson Phi'
Imperial College
Royston Gree
University of A

PROFESSIONAL OCCUPATIONS AND ORGANIZATIONS

Daniel Muzio
University of York
Sundeep Aulakh
University of Leeds
Ian Kirkpatrick
University of York

CAMBRIDGE
UNIVERSITY PRESS

CAMBRIDGE
UNIVERSITY PRESS

University Printing House, Cambridge CB2 8BS, United Kingdom

One Liberty Plaza, 20th Floor, New York, NY 10006, USA

477 Williamstown Road, Port Melbourne, VIC 3207, Australia

314–321, 3rd Floor, Plot 3, Splendor Forum, Jasola District Centre,
New Delhi – 110025, India

79 Anson Road, #06–04/06, Singapore 079906

Cambridge University Press is part of the University of Cambridge.

It furthers the University's mission by disseminating knowledge in the pursuit of
education, learning, and research at the highest international levels of excellence.

www.cambridge.org
Information on this title: www.cambridge.org/9781108789851
DOI: 10.1017/9781108804318

First published 2019

A catalogue record for this publication is available from the British Library.

ISBN 978-1-108-78985-1 Paperback
ISSN 2397-947X (online)
ISSN 2514-3859 (print)

Professional Occupations and Organizations

Elements in Organization Theory

DOI: 10.1017/9781108804318
First published online: December 2019

Daniel Muzio
University of York

Sundeep Aulakh
University of Leeds

Ian Kirkpatrick
University of York

Author for correspondence: Daniel Muzio, daniel.muzio@york.ac.uk

Abstract: In this Element, we engage with fundamental questions concerning the future trajectory of professions as a distinct occupational category and of the formal organizations which represent, employ or host professionals. We begin with a literature review that identifies a functionalist, power and institutionalist lens for the study of professional occupations and organizations. We then review a series of challenges which face the contemporary professions. Finally, we explore contemporary developments in the worlds of professions applying three units of analysis: macro (professional occupations and their associations), meso (professional organizations) and micro (professional workers).

Keywords: professional organizations, professional occupations, professionals, professional services firms, sociology of the professions

ISBNs: 9781108789851 (PB) 9781108804318 (OC)
ISSNs: 2397-947X (online) 2514-3859 (print)

Contents

1 An Introduction and Overview

1.1 Introduction

As Andrew Abbott famously stated, professions 'heal our bodies, measure our profits and save our souls' (1988: 1). This quote neatly captures the influence and pervasiveness of professions and professionals in our world. In Europe, the roots of many modern-day professions can be traced back to the nineteenth century or earlier, especially with regard to the archetypal cases of medicine, law, academia and the clergy. These professions bore many of the hallmarks of medieval craft guilds, which focused narrowly on protecting the monopolies of skilled trades (Krause, 1996), but also Gesellschaft forms of association, emphasizing scientific inquiry and a universalistic orientation (Adler et al., 2008). From these foundations, a more significant expansion of professions took place in the twentieth century as knowledge became more specialized and demand for expertise grew in a wider range of fields. This process led to the emergence of new occupations (e.g. scientists, engineers, teachers, project managers and many more) claiming professional recognition and status, a trend that continues to this day. In the USA, for example, the steady expansion of the professional and technical occupations has resulted in this category becoming the largest occupational group, employing 30 million people and representing 21 per cent of the workforce in 2016, compared to 12 per cent in 1965 (BLS, 2016; 1965).

These trends highlight the continued growth of a professional workforce with distinctive characteristics (Leicht & Fennell, 2001). The number, size and sophistication of organizations that directly employ or play host to professionals or claim to represent them (membership associations) has also grown exponentially. These organizations include professional bureaucracies such as hospitals, schools and universities that remain central to the operation of the welfare state and delivery of public services to large populations (Ackroyd et al., 2007). Equally significant are professional services firms (PSFs), which are amongst the largest, most complex and most globally diversified organizations in the contemporary economy (Empson et al., 2015).

There can be little doubt, then, that professionals and their organizations matter. Yet, in recent years, a growing number of scholars have raised questions about the ubiquity and authority of the professions, with some predicting their demise (Reed, 2007; Leicht, 2016). There are several strands to this debate. Some draw attention to deskilling and de-professionalization risks due to the enhanced possibilities of information technology and managerialism (Arronowitz & DiFazio, 1995; Susskind & Susskind, 2015). It is sometimes argued that professionals are facing their own industrial revolution as mass production methods replace craft-based production. Others emphasize ways in which neo-liberal government agendas have unsettled traditional regulatory arrangements and, by infusing distinctively commercial and managerial logics, are reshaping the professions (Brock et al., 1999).

The complexity of problems confronting society and changes in consumer demand for professional services represent a further set of challenges (Noordegraaf, 2011). Traditionally, highly specialized professional knowledge has focused on individual case treatment: curing patients, teaching pupils and balancing the books. However, it is argued that the 'wicked' nature of many contemporary social problems, such as those relating to climate change or population ageing, now requires a pooling of expertise and greater collaboration. In areas such as health, this threatens to undermine existing professional jurisdictions and the established status hierarchy to provide services that are both interdisciplinary and co-produced with users (Ferlie et al., 2011; Adler & Kwon, 2013).

Lastly, observers have focused on the legitimacy crisis facing professionals, amplified by several high-profile instances of professional malpractice (Reed, 1996; Muzio et al., 2016; Gabbioneta et al., 2018; Dixon-Woods et al., 2011). This 'dark side' of the professions is apparent in areas such as healthcare, symbolized by the Shipman affair in the UK National Health Service (NHS) and the Kennedy Inquiry into unwarranted child mortality at Bristol Royal Infirmary (Saks, 2015). A number of high-profile corporate scandals such as Enron and Parmalat (Gabbioneta et al., 2013; 2014) have also shaken public confidence. These could only occur with the acquiescence, if not complicity, of the very professional advisors who, in theory, should have prevented such misbehaviour. Indeed, in the words of Mitchell and Sikka (2011: 8): 'scratch the surface of any financial scandal or a tax dodge and the invisible hand of major accountancy firms is highly evident'.

Hence, questions arise as to how far the established mode of professional self-regulation and organization can be maintained in light of these challenges. On the one hand, it seems that many professional occupations are on a journey towards de-professionalization. However, as will be discussed, the resilient and adaptable nature of the professions should not be underestimated. In this regard, the future may witness not so much a decline but a 'reconfiguration' of the professions and professional (or community) forms of organizing (Adler et al., 2008).

In this Element, we engage with these fundamental questions concerning the future trajectory of the professions, their organizations and members. However, prior to doing so, it is important to clarify some key terms of reference and boundary conditions that will shape our analysis (also see Table 1 for a summary of key terms). First is to distinguish between 'professionalism' as an analytical, social category and one employed as a rhetorical resource (Muzio & Kirkpatrick, 2011). It is clear that the words 'profession' and 'professionalism' can also have wider significance. This partly arises from a semantic confusion surrounding their usage in the English language. Sometimes the word 'profession' is used as a polite synonym for work, job or occupation (for example, 'what is your job or profession?'). This discursive dimension of professionalism has become more important in recent years. Claims to be 'professional' may originate 'from below' by individuals, occupations and organizations to signal their quality and status but can also be deployed 'from above' by managers and employers to elicit commitment, maintain control and justify processes of occupational or organizational change (Fournier, 1999; Evetts, 2014). However, our primary focus in this Element will be on professionalism as a 'social category', a distinct mode of labour market organization whereby members of an occupation (rather than consumers or employers) retain control over the definition, performance and evaluation of their work (Freidson 2001; Brint, 1994).

A second key assumption that will guide our analysis concerns the relationship between 'occupations' and 'professions'. At its simplest, an 'occupation' signifies a community of practitioners with similar skill requirements engaging in common work tasks that are relatively enduring, either within a sector or spanning several sectors (Anteby et al., 2016). While administrative categories – such as the standard occupational classification system (or SOC) – represent a useful starting point, the way occupations are defined and labelled is socially constructed and fluid (Bechky, 2003). In some cases, this leads to the institutionalization of 'occupational communities' (Van Maanen & Barley, 1984) that 'shape our individual identities, tastes, and affiliations' (Bechky, 2011: 1158). By contrast, a profession is a more specific category. According to Ritzer and Walczak (1986: 44), a profession is 'an occupation that has had the power to have undergone a development process enabling it to acquire or convince significant others' and 'has acquired a constellation of characteristics we have come to accept as denoting a profession'.

A third area where it is important to define terms of reference is with regard to the notion of professional organizations (Muzio & Kirkpatrick, 2011). Although this term is frequently used in the literature, its precise meaning is not always clear. This is partly due to a historical divide between the 'sociology of professions and occupations' and 'sociology of organizations' (Lounsbury & Kaghan, 2001). While the former draws attention to professionalism as a distinctive way of organizing in the labour market (as already mentioned), the latter is concerned with the organizations that represent, employ or play host to professionals. Nevertheless, even within the specific 'sociology of organizations' there is often some confusion. According to Scott (1965: 65), 'professional organizations' are those in which 'members of one or more professional groups play the central role in the achievement of the primary organizational objectives'. However, within this broad category, further distinctions are necessary. The first is between organizations that directly employ or play host to practising professionals and 'membership-based organizations' (Hudson et al., 2013) which represent them. A second distinction is within the category of organizations that employ or play host to professionals, between so-called *autonomous* and *heteronomous* organizations. The former consists of organizations where professionals *own or control core assets* (Empson et al., 2015), such as in the case of law, accounting and management consulting firms (Powell et al., 1999). By contrast, the latter refer to situations where professionals are employed (or contracted) within a wider bureaucratic structure and are subject to external control but lack any distinct organizational identity. Typical examples include public service agencies (schools, universities, hospitals), although this category might also encompass professional departments (such as human resources or finance) within large multi-divisional corporations.

A final set of assumptions made in this Element concern the cultural and historical specificity of notions of professionalism (Sciulli, 2005). As we shall see, much of the literature depicts professions as collective agents, operating relatively autonomously in civil society in pursuit of distinctive strategies or goals. However, this perspective has deep roots in the Anglo-American historical context, emphasizing 'the freedom of self-employed practitioners to control work conditions' (Collins, 1990: 98). By contrast, in France, where the state 'restricted the autonomy of the institutions of civil society', professional development followed a different path (MacDonald 1995: 97). Here, according to MacDonald: 'knowledge-based services have remained in the ambit of the state, restricting the success of the professional project' (MacDonald 1995: 97). Similarly, McClelland (1991) distinguishes between a 'professionalization from above' and a 'professionalization from below' pattern. The former is especially relevant to state socialist or post-communist societies, including China, where even high-status expert groups such as doctors remain effectively state functionaries. Therefore, while the notion of professions and professionalization has (arguably increasing) global relevance, one must also acknowledge certain cultural and historical biases, which underpin much of the literature on this topic.

1.2 Structure of the Element

In what follows, we build on the aforementioned distinctions to address some of the central questions concerning the nature and future trajectory of professions as a distinct occupational category and of professional *organizations*. To accomplish our goals, the Element unfolds over six additional chapters. In Sections 2 and 3, we focus on the theoretical underpinnings of research on the professions and contemporary challenges. Section 2 reviews key approaches to the study of professional occupations and organizations through three distinct lenses: function, power and institution. These lenses present substantially different understandings of professionalism, which have unfolded chronologically. Section 3 then assesses three challenges facing contemporary professions: cultural delegitimization, the disruptive potential of new technologies and changing regulation.

Building on these debates, we explore contemporary developments in the worlds of professions applying three units of analysis: *macro, meso* and *micro*. Starting at the macro level, Section 4 focuses on the increasing role of professions and their associations in regulating occupations and labour markets. Section 5 (meso) turns to the rise in the size, influence and sophistication of professional organizations in both public and private sectors. Lastly, Section 6 considers how the lived experience of work is changing, raising questions about professional autonomy and identity. We note that, whilst the effects of macroeconomic and societal forces have, undoubtedly, altered the lived experience of professional work, professionals have proven to be highly adept at developing strategies to respond to emergent challenges and exploiting the opportunities presented by them (Evetts, 2011). In each chapter, we provide an overview of substantive debates drawing on a wide range of secondary sources. We conclude by discussing various scenarios regarding the future of the professional occupations and organizations and suggesting some directions for additional research.

1.3 A Summary of Key Terms

This section has introduced several core terms relating to professions and professional organizations that are integral to the discussion in the rest of the Element. For quick reference, definitions are summarized in Table 1.

2 Three Lenses for Studying Professional Occupations and Organizations

2.1 Introduction

This section provides an overview of the theoretical literature on professions. Key concepts and debates within the sociology of professions and organization theory are reviewed and classified, using *three* distinct lenses: function, power and institutions. Broadly, these lenses follow the historical evolution of theory

Table 1 A Summary of Key Terms

Term	Definition	More detail ...
Occupation	An occupation refers to a community of practitioners with similar skill requirements engaging in common work tasks that are relatively enduring, either within a sector or spanning several sectors.	
Profession	An occupation that has undergone several stages of development and successfully effected tactics and strategies that convinced others (especially the state and public) to accord it the status of a 'profession' with resultant material and social benefits.	Throughout, but see Section 2 for debate on definition.
Professionalism	An analytical category denoting a distinct mode of labour market organization whereby members of an occupation (rather than consumers or employers) retain a high degree of control over the definition, performance and evaluation of their work.	Throughout, but see Section 2, 4 and 6 for challenges and adaptations.
Professionalization	The process that leads to professionalism. Sometimes this is referred to as a 'professional project' aimed at negotiating labour market shelters and upward social mobility.	As above, but especially Section 4.
Membership-based organizations.	Formal organizations (such as professional associations) whose remit centres on advancing the interests of its members collectively with a view to (but not always) acquiring or maintaining the status of a 'profession' and access to market and cultural benefits.	See Section 4.

Table 1 (cont.)

Term	Definition	More detail ...
Autonomous organizations	Organizations where professionals own or control core assets, resulting in a unique governance style and high practitioner autonomy. Professional Services Firms are an archetypal example.	See Section 5
Professional service firms	Private sector organizations which are characterized by: knowledge intensity, low capital intensity and a professionalized workforce (Von Nordenflycht, 2010).	See Section 5
Professional workers	A distinct category of workers (employed or self-employed) whose work entails the application of theoretical and scientific knowledge to individual cases. The terms and conditions of work traditionally command considerable autonomy from external oversight, except by peer representatives.	See Section 5

and research on the professions, which originated in the 1930s (Gorman & Sandefur, 2011; Muzio et al., 2013). Each lens includes several perspectives, often with different theoretical foundations, but all share a distinct understanding of professionalism as an occupational ideology and work organization method. See Table 2 for an overview.

Unsurprisingly, specific issues may look very different according to which lens one adopts. Thus, from a functionalist lens, the 'up or out' promotion system typical of large accountancy and law firms (see Section 6) is justified by the need to promote the most skilled and dedicated staff. By contrast, a 'power' lens views it as a device to further the interests of professional elites by encouraging processes of work intensification (Ackroyd & Muzio, 2007). As such, the three lenses are analytically distinct, rooted in different theoretical perspectives, research traditions and, in some cases, incompatible understandings of professions and their role in society.

In what follows, we first explore what the three lenses imply for broader understandings of the professions. Later, we examine how they have been

Table 2 Three Lenses for Studying Professions

	Functional	**Power**	**Institution**
Sociological Theory	Functionalist sociology	Weberian and Marxist sociology, including social closure theory, labour process theory and Foucouldian-inspired perspectives	Institutional theory
Primary Focus	Function of professions as (largely) altruistic sources of social solidarity and cohesion	Professions as self-interested agents engaged in 'pro-fessionalization projects' Professions as agents and sub-jects of control	Role of professions as cultural producers in shaping organizational fields and societal institutions
Understanding of Professions	Distinctive traits of professional occupations	Professionalization as a process	Professions as institutions
Key Exemplars	Carr-Saunders and Wilson (1933); Goode (1957); Wilensky (1964)	Abbott (1988); Freidson (1988; 1994); Johnson (1972); Larson (1977)	Scott (2008); Thornton et al. (2012); Muzio et al. (2013)

applied to theories of professional organizations whilst noting that the literature in this area is still evolving.

2.2 Functionalist Lens

Functionalist accounts of professionalism begin with Emile Durkheim, who, like others after him, was preoccupied with the issue of social cohesion. Arguing that capitalism generates moral anarchy and would self-destruct unless it is contained within a society defined by mutual interest (1992: 23–5), Durkheim singles out the 'professional grouping' as 'a moral force capable of curbing individual egoism' (1984: xxxix). He explains that self-regulating occupational communities foster a sense of solidarity and moral responsibility by socializing members to focus not on their own self-interest but on that of the whole community (Durkheim, 1992). Others, such as Carr-Saunders and Wilson (1933), identify professionalism as a force for stability and freedom against the apparent threat of industrial and governmental bureaucracies.

Hence, the functionalist lens emphasizes the altruistic motives of professions and the intrinsic value of their expertise to public welfare. According to T. H. Marshall, professionalism 'is not concerned with self-interest, but with the welfare of the client' (1939: 331–2), such that the professional 'does not work in order to be paid: he is paid in order that he may work' (325). More recently, this has been associated with what Schneyer (2013) terms the 'business/profession dichotomy'. While business people are motivated only by profit, professionals, it is argued, are driven by altruism and notions of public trusteeship. Indeed, it is often claimed that professional values are still a critically important bulwark against the worst abuses of the free market. Anteby (2010), for example, shows how even trades that are morally questionable – such as dealing in human cadavers in the USA – may acquire legitimacy when sanctioned by professionals.

From this perspective, the common traits of professions, such as labour market monopoly and self-regulation, are necessary and in the public interest (Parsons, 1954). For instance, barriers to entry (monopoly) may be in the public interest by guaranteeing high standards of education and training of licensed practitioners (Halliday, 1987). In this way, the unqualified and incompetent are excluded, the safety of the public assured, and the quality of services enhanced. A similar argument is made about ethical codes and rules that have sought to insulate practitioners from competition (Merton, 1982).

2.2.1 'Traits-Based' Models of the Professions

'Traits-based' models of the professions, which grew in influence in the 1950s, constitute another characteristic of the functionalist approach. These models sought to identify the unique attributes of 'professional' occupations in order to make explicit what sets them apart from other expert and non-expert workers (Muzio et al., 2013). Goode (1957) for instance, identified eight characterizing features of profession, which included, amongst others, a lifelong calling, common identity and compliance with an ethical code. In a systematic review of this literature, Hickson and Thomas (1969) identified twenty different models, including fourteen mutually exclusive traits.

Other scholars have built on this approach to explore professions at different stages of development, for example Etzioni's (1969) classic distinction between professions and so-called semi professions. Traits models also became associated with the idea of an ideal-typical life cycle – involving key stages of development whereby certain occupations develop over time. Wilensky (1964) famously noted seven stages that (historically) characterized the formation of both established and newer professional occupations. These stages included: becoming a full-time occupation; opening a training school and then a university course; establishing a formal association (regionally and nationally); achieving state recognition through licensing; and signing up to a formal code of ethics.

Traits models have been highly influential in defining the boundary conditions of 'professions' (Leblebici & Sherer, 2015). However, by the late 1960s, functionalist accounts were beginning to lose their appeal. Traits-based scholarship came to be seen as a misguided focus of sociological enquiry, not least because it was largely ahistorical and failed to explain the power of particular occupational groups (Evetts, 2014). It transpired that many lists (of traits) were based on an idealized view, drawn from the exemplar professions of the nineteenth century: law and medicine. Critics also argued that the taxonomic approach was oriented more towards legitimizing professional ideologies as opposed to depicting them in practice (Saks, 2016).

2.3 Power Lens

From the mid-1960s, attention shifted from studying professions as occupations with shared traits to professionalization as a *process* (Suddaby & Muzio, 2015). This involved reframing the sociology of the professions away from the old question 'what is a profession' towards a concern with how occupations accomplish and maintain professional status. As Everett C. Hughes (1963) famously stated: 'in my studies I passed from the false question "Is this occupation a profession' to the more fundamental one "what are the circumstances in which people in an occupation attempt to turn it into a profession and themselves into professional people?"' Accordingly, the focus moved towards trying to understand how occupations accomplished professionalism as a strategic and purposeful endeavour (Becker, 1970) and away from producing checklists of the definitive traits deemed to constitute a 'profession'.

This shift in thinking reinforced the centrality of power for understanding professions. Specifically, it meant focusing on professionalization as a process whereby an occupation gains control over a work jurisdiction. Hence, Johnson (1972) noted how, in theory, any occupation might seek to mobilize knowledge to gain monopoly control over expert work and the power that this affords. From this perspective, professionalism is defined as 'a peculiar type of occupational control rather than an expression of the inherent nature of particular occupations' (Johnson, 1972: 45). In its most developed form, professionalism grants producers' control over the definition, execution, regulation, evaluation and remuneration of their own work, what Freidson (1988) terms 'occupational dominance'.

The power lens, therefore, steers us in a different direction from earlier functionalist accounts. Professionalism emerges as a distinct ideology and method of work organization in which *any* aspiring occupation might achieve a significant degree of control over the definition, execution and evaluation of its work (Freidson, 1994). In stark contrast to functionalist accounts, the power lens also maintains a 'healthy scepticism' for professional claims of moral superiority (Crompton, 1990).

To further illustrate these ideas, we now consider *two* influential strands of work in more detail that draw firstly on Weberian and, secondly, on Marxian and to a lesser extent Foucauldian theory respectively. While the former highlights the centrality of 'professionalization projects' and the objectives of 'occupational closure', the latter focuses more on the relationships between professions, the state and large corporations and their role as both *agents* and *subjects* of control and governmentality.

2.3.1 The Professional Project

A central tenant of the Weberian sociology of professions is the notion of a 'professional project' (Larson, 1977). This refers to the systematic and deliberate attempts by the professions to 'translate a scarce set of cultural and technical resources into a secure and institutionalized system of social and financial rewards' (Larson, 1977: xvii). The assumed goal of all projects is 'occupational closure' (Murphy, 1986; Parkin, 1974), allowing professions to maintain skill scarcity and maximize rewards 'by restricting access to rewards and opportunities to a limited circle of eligibles' (Parkin, 1974: 3). This often takes the form of credentialization (Collins, 1990), where access to a profession depends on the acquisition of formal (university-level) qualifications and certificates, which signal expertise. Implied is that credentials act as a mechanism to maintain monopolies around specific jurisdictions and to regulate the supply of labour within these (Abel, 1988). The purpose is primarily economic, as closure, by limiting supply, can generate higher economic rents and maximize the returns associated with professional membership. However, rewards may also be symbolic, as closure may increase the prestige, social standing and intrinsic benefits of professions (MacDonald, 1995). Thus, in Larson's words: 'the double nature of the professional project intertwines market and status orientations, and both tend towards monopoly – monopoly of opportunities for income in a market of services, on the one hand, and monopoly of status in an emerging occupational hierarchy, on the other' (Larson 1977: xiii, xiv).

Building on this idea, MacDonald (1995: 29–34) notes how professionalization projects are enacted simultaneously in both the 'economic' and 'social' orders. The former relates to the collective effort (by occupational associations or other bodies) to gain control over the process of knowledge production and the training and education of new entrants: what Abel (1988) terms the 'production of producers'. This depends on how far aspiring professions are able to strike a 'regulative bargain' with the state (MacDonald, 1995). These bargains usually result in the creation of 'labour market shelters' (Timmermans, 2008) that offer protection from competition, for instance, in the form of state licensing and registration, or Royal Charters in the UK (see Section 4.3). Turning to the social order, much depends on the ability of professions to mobilize support, validating claims of closure and their privileged status. Such claims may relate to the efficacy of their 'technical competence' (Collins, 1990) or, more broadly, to discourses of social trusteeship that justify professional monopoly as being in the public interest (Brint, 1994).

The focus on professionalization projects substantially broadens the field of inquiry beyond elite groups such as law, medicine or academia to include *any* aspiring group seeking to establish an 'occupational mandate' (Fayard et al., 2017). It also draws attention to the wider ecology of professions and relationships between groups engaged in competing 'projects'. This idea is central to Abbott's (1988) notion of a 'system of professions', where jurisdictional boundaries between professions, which are equipped with alternative forms of abstract knowledge, are in constant flux. In this 'system', the nature of occupational strategies may vary depending on the position of each group (Witz, 1991). While dominant occupations – such as medicine – may focus primarily on 'exclusionary' and demarcation strategies, subordinate groups are focused on upward mobility projects to enhance their position and status. Either way, the implication is that, in a 'system of professions' subject to 'constant jostling and readjustment' (Abbott, 1988: 33), no professional claim is ever entirely stable or free from challenge.

In most areas, this 'system' also has a strong gendered dimension. For example, in healthcare, we see the emergence of a highly gendered division of labour between professions, with male-dominated groups (such as medicine) at the pinnacle of the status hierarchy and women corralled and socialized into subordinate or auxiliary professions such as nursing, midwifery and social work (Witz, 1991). A similar picture applies in the corporate world, such as law and accounting firms, where partners are predominantly male whilst salaried associates and supporting occupations are mainly female (Anderson-Gough et al., 2005; Bolton & Muzio, 2008). Thus, the power lens explains how professions display increasing levels of inequality and vertical stratification.

Although the 1970s and 1980s marked the heyday of Weberian perspectives, this approach remains influential (Saks, 2016). One strand in particular has sought to refine notions of occupational closure and ways in which these apply to the professions (Weeden & Grusky, 2014). A notable example is Weeden's (2002) distinction between four primary mechanisms of occupational closure: membership of associations, credentializing (higher educational qualifications); voluntary certification; and state licensing (and other forms of state regulation). The first three represent *soft* forms of closure, or an 'open market form of regulation', which achieves a modicum of protection for aspiring professions (and their clients) without strong state backing (Lester, 2016: 2). By contrast, licensing implies a harder 'state-sanctioned quasi-monopoly' (Freidson, 1994: 83). As explored in Section 4, in the USA licensing is widely imposed at city, state or even federal levels, circumscribing the 'right to practice' and the use of occupational titles (e.g. Dentist, Lawyer) (Law and Kim, 2005). According to Weeden (2002), professions are often the principal actors negotiating these forms of closure. They do so through four related activities: restricting supply; enhancing overall demand for expert credentials or skills; channelling that demand to specific occupations (as sole providers); and signalling to external gatekeepers the value and efficacy of professional expertise.

2.3.2 Professions as Agents and Subjects of Control

A related strand of work that falls within the power lens on professions are those influenced directly or indirectly by Marxist and (to a lesser extent) Foucauldian ideas (Macdonald, 1995; Torstendahl, 1990). A starting point for the former is the idea that professional formation is bound up with wider social and economic processes, especially those associated with capitalist relations of production (Hanlon, 1998). From this perspective, the development of professions and their ability to negotiate autonomy must be understood in relation to prevailing structural conditions. The purposeful action of professions (as already explained) represents a necessary but not sufficient condition for professional formation. Marxist and Foucauldian approaches also highlight the ongoing challenges to professional autonomy, linked to the demands of the capitalist labour process (or the state-centred governmentality projects) to maximize efficiency through encroaching bureaucratic control.

The work of Terry Johnson provides one of the earliest and most developed examples of this approach (1972; 1977; 1982). Although concerned with the agency of professions, Johnson (1972) was also keen to highlight the structural conditions under which different forms of professionalism might flourish. These conditions include the extent to which power and information asymmetries separate producers from consumers and how these imbalances are resolved. Hence, 'collegial' professionalism arose when producers were more knowledgeable, resourceful, organized and coherent than their consumers. By contrast, 'corporate patronage' professions emerged when imbalances were not so significant or where they favoured the consumers of professional services such as large corporate clients. Finally, 'state-mediated' professionalism occurred when the state intervened to regulate asymmetries within a particular producer/consumer exchange, such as in health or education.

Johnson's account implies a recursive, coevolving relationship between the professions (as semi-autonomous agents) and other key actors, including large corporations and especially the state. He notes that 'as a historical process, the professions are emergent as a condition of state formation and state formation is a major condition of professional autonomy – where such exists'. (Johnson, 1982: 189). Viewed in this way, the autonomy of professional groups, such as doctors, arises in a large part from their technical expertise and their ability to solve problems and manage risks on behalf of powerful consumers (including the state) (Johnson, 1977). As Cousins also suggests, 'as functional groups, professional provider groups are drawn into a specific relationship with the state in order to formulate and implement public policies' (1987: 106). This ensures that they are granted 'structurally determined privileges' such as greater autonomy, status and employment security – although these 'privileges' vary between groups depending on their status.

In the corporate world, very similar dynamics have shaped the relative power and autonomy of professions within management (Leicht & Fennell, 2001). Here, too, the formation and development of professions is regarded as being contingent on their ability to control 'high value added applications' and 'work that is closely related to profit potentials, critical environmental uncertainties, or managerial effectiveness' (Brint, 1994: 73). This idea is central to the work of Peter Armstrong (2000), who focuses on the competition for influence between accountancy and other organizational professionals (such as personnel managers). According to Armstrong, in the United Kingdom the dominant position of accountants can be explained by the perceived superior functionality of their expert knowledge in being able to control the labour process – management's central objective.

A further development of the idea comes from the work of Michel Foucault (1977), suggesting that professions form part of the 'apparatus of governmentality' (Gane & Johnson, 1993: 143). According to this view, the state represents an 'ensemble of institutions, procedures, tactics, calculations, knowledge and technologies, which together comprise the particular direction the government has taken' (140). Professional knowledge is central to the state's capacity to ensure governmentality, assisting with surveillance, discipline and normalization of citizens' behaviour in areas such as public and mental health, education and policing. In the corporate world, the power knowledge discourses of professionals such as accountants and human resources managers perform a similar control (or governance) function with regard to clients and employees (Townley, 1994).

A related strand of work influenced by Marxist (and Foucauldian) theory relates to how professions themselves might also become *subjects* of control. Interest in this topic has been long-standing, with early accounts of the professions highlighting a fundamental tension between the ideals of professional autonomy and bureaucracy (Hall, 1968). However, in the 1970s, this debate was given a further boost with the addition of ideas from labour process theory (Braverman, 1974) and notions of proletarianization (Oppenheimer, 1973). The latter draws attention to how professionals are subject to the same processes of routinization, rationalization, commodification and deskilling that apply to other groups in the workforce (Haug, 1972). These tendencies mean that 'bureaucracy replaces in the professionals' own work place factory-like conditions' (Oppenheimer 1973: 214). Over time, while some professionals may gain power, others will lose their status as independent practitioners, suffering a 'loss of control over decisions concerning the goals, objectives and policy directions of … work' (Derber, 1982: 18).

As discussed in Sections 3 and 6, arguments about the long-term demise of the professions remain influential, with more recent accounts giving particular attention to the role of technology (Susskind & Susskind, 2015). This idea has also influenced accounts of PSFs as organizations that engage in increasingly sophisticated forms of identity regulation through technologies and power knowledge discourses aimed at disciplining and controlling individual professionals (Anderson-Gough et al., 2000; Covaleski et al., 1998). At this point, however, it is important only to note how these assumptions relate to what we loosely term a 'power' lens on the professions. A core idea is that, while professions have been successful to varying degrees in negotiating autonomy within the ambit of the state and large corporations, they are not immune from the same processes of control (and proletarianization) which they themselves have helped to unleash.

2.4 The Institution Lens

Despite its merits and lasting influence, the 'power' lens on the sociology of the professions has been criticized for placing too much emphasis on the narrow objective of achieving occupational control (or closure) as the sole driving force (and outcome) of contemporary professionalism. Whilst this was a necessary corrective to the apolitical and largely power-blind nature of the functional lens, subsequent researchers have emphasized how professional action may also be guided by broader concerns than narrow economic self-interest (Crompton, 1990). Thus, by analysing archival sources, Terrence Halliday's (1987) study of the Chicago Bar Association reveals that only a small minority of the professions' time is concerned with monopoly and closure whilst the majority of its resources are directed towards public-oriented issues such as the efficient administration of justice. Overall, a substantial body of knowledge indicates how, 'in many cases the advancement of professional interests is not inconsistent with attention to client welfare' (Scott, 2008: 221).

Whilst no single framework has displaced the power lens, institutional theory presents a particularly fruitful lens for reconceptualizing the study of the professions (Scott, 2008; Muzio et al., 2013; Suddaby & Muzio, 2015). Sociologist Kevin Leicht captures this position most explicitly: 'recent theoretical development in the professions focuses on the rise and dominance of the professions as institutions. Professions as macro-level institutions represent distinctive and identifiable structures of knowledge, expertise, work and labour markets with distinct norms, practices, ideologies and organizational forms' (2005: 604). We explore this assertion more fully next, looking first at how professions might be understood *as* institutions and, second, how they are more broadly associated with the formation and transformation of societal institutions.

2.4.1 Professions as Institutions

An early and dominant meaning given to institutionalization is one where 'social processes, obligations or actualities come to take a rule-like status in social thought and action' (Meyer & Rowan, 1977: 341). Because the professions are 'widely followed, without debate and exhibit permanence' (Greenwood et al., 2008: 5), they, too, can be regarded as 'institutions'. Rooted in history that stretches back to pre-modernity (Krause, 1996; Sciulli, 2005), the professions have, over time, evolved to become so firmly embedded in the fabric of social life that relying on the services of certified experts is, in many cases, natural and unquestioned.

The 'professions', therefore, represent a core societal institution, with a distinct logic. An institutional logic refers to the 'socially constructed, historical patterns of material practices, assumptions, values, beliefs, and rules by which individuals produce and reproduce their material subsistence, organize time and

Table 3 Institutional Logics of Societal Sectors

	Markets	**Corporations**	**Professions**
Source of identity	Faceless	Bureaucratic role	Professional association Personal reputation
Source of legitimacy	Share price	Market position	Personal expertise
Source of authority	Shareholder activism	Board of directors	Professional association
Basis of norms	Self-interest	Employment in firm	Membership of professional association
Basis of strategy	Increase efficiency	Increase size	Increase quality of service
Control mechanisms	Regulation	Board and management authority	Peer review

Source: Abridged and adapted from Thornton et al. (2012: 56)

space, and provide meaning to their social reality' (Thornton & Ocasio, 1999: 804). An early account of the specific features of the professional logic was produced in Thornton and Ocasio's 1999 paper on higher education publishing and has since been developed in subsequent research projects. This is reproduced in an abridged form in Table 3 and contrasted with alternative logics associated with the market and the corporation.

When focusing on professional 'logics' it is important to acknowledge three things. First, the organizing principles are ideal-typical in nature. Second, these principles may vary between organizational fields; for example, a publisher's professional logic will differ from an accountant's. Finally, organizing principles may differ from one historical and cultural context to another (Faulconbridge & Muzio, 2016).

2.5 Professionalization as Institutionalization

Building on this idea that professions are exemplar 'institutions', it has been argued that professionalization also represents a process of institutionalization (Suddaby and Viale, 2011; Muzio et al., 2013). Here, professionalization is viewed as 'a particular flavour of the broader category of institutionalization insofar as it represents one of several ways to give order, structure and meaning to a distinctive area of social and economic life (the production of expertise)' (Muzio et al., 2013: 705). Viewed in this way, all 'professional projects carry with them projects of institutionalization'. As actors pursue their professionalization projects, inevitably their efforts 'reverberate through the field' (Suddaby & Viale, 2011: 423, 426) and impact on surrounding institutions. As such, one of the crucial aspects of the emergent (ecological) institutional lens is that, whilst professions are deemed to be in competition with other occupations *and* related institutions, professionalization projects are only likely to be (or remain) successful if strategically aligned 'with a related and symbiotic project of institutionalization' involving other key actors (Suddaby & Muzio, 2015: 36). Clearly, this raises the question as to which institutionalization project counts as 'related'. Uppermost, at least historically, this has been the project of the nation state, as discussed in Section 2.3 under the 'power lens' (Johnson, 1972; Gane & Johnson, 1993). Yet, more recently, allegiances have shifted towards the large corporation (Suddaby & Muzio, 2015). According to Suddaby et al. (2007: 334), 'the historical regulatory bargain between professional associations and nation states is being superseded by a new compact between conglomerate professional and transnational trade organizations'.

2.5.1 The Agency of the Professions: Institutional Work and Entrepreneurship

Studying professional occupations and organizations through an institutionalist lens also alerts us to their agency and broader societal role. DiMaggio and Powell (1983) view professionals as the principal source of normative isomorphism, pushing organizations within fields to converge around shared structures and practices. This occurs because professionals 'exhibit much similarity to their counterparts in other organizations' (152). As professionals carry with them strong and consistent expectations of how a particular function, such as finance, marketing or purchasing, should be organized, they act as a powerful 'vehicle for the definition and promulgation of normative rules about organizational and professional behaviour' (DiMaggio & Powell, 1991: 71) both within and across fields.

While early accounts highlight the role of professions in reproducing institutions, recent attention has been given to agency and institutional entrepreneurship (Hardy & McGuire, 2008). The agentic role of the professions was developed most fully by Scott (2008) in his characterization of professions as the 'Lords of the Dance' of institutional change. He states, '[T]he professions in modern society have assumed leading roles in the creation and tending of institutions. They are the preeminent institutional agents of our time' (Scott,

2008: 219). Using the 'pillars of institutionalism' as a framework, Scott elaborates upon three resources through which the professions exercise this role: regulative, normative and cognitive-cultural. The cognitive-cultural refers to the role of the professions in producing knowledge frameworks and solutions that define how particular issues (such as healthcare or engineering) are conceived and addressed. By contrast, the normative refers to the ability of the professions to generate a sense of moral obligation by defining what is right and proper. Finally, the regulative refers to the ability to rely on the coercive power of legally sanctionable rules. Whilst this applies to all professions benefiting from a state-sanctioned monopoly (see Section 2.3.1), it is most pronounced amongst those involved in the exercise of state power such as the police, the military, law and the judiciary.

Scott's framework opened the way to further efforts to better understand the institutional role of the professions. Examples include Suddaby and Viale (2011) and Muzio et al. (2013), who draw on the notion of 'institutional work' (Lawrence & Suddaby, 2006) to delineate a multi-stage cycle through which professions *create, maintain* and *disrupt* institutions. Thus, in Suddaby and Viale's (2011) terms, professions begin by creating or taking over new jurisdictions (Abbott, 1988). Such projects have inevitably broader systemic effects as they affect surrounding institutions. An example of this is DiMaggio's (1991) study of the professional project of museum curators, which in its process redefined the very concept of the museum shifting this from private to public ownership. Second, professions populate jurisdictions with new actors. These include new organizational forms – such as multi-functional forms of business (Fligstein, 1990), multi-hospital integrated healthcare systems (Scott et al., 2000) or, indeed, the national public museum (DiMaggio, 1991) – as well as new occupational groups such as recycling managers or environmental officers (Hoffman, 1999; Lounsbury, 2001), all of which have significant effects on the nature of broader organizational fields. Third, professions help to redraw the rules and boundaries of existing fields. Examples include the re-scaling of national jurisdictions into transnational ones (Faulconbridge & Muzio, 2016; Samsonova-Taddei & Humphrey, 2014) and the capture of processes of international arbitration by global law firms (Dezalay & Garth, 1996). Finally, professions control access and advancement within fields through practices such as up-or-out promotion systems (Galanter & Palay, 1991), tenure tracks (Park et al., 2011), pupillages (Siebert et al., 2016) or formal dining requirements (Dacin et al., 2010). These practices have important implications for career structures, social mobility and social stratification (Tomlinson et al., 2013; 2018; Gorman, 2005; 2015).

An institutionalist lens has the potential to make a number of distinct contributions to the study of the professions. First, unlike the power and functionalist lenses, it notes how professional agencies are neither guided wholly by self- or public interest but may engage with both objectives. Second, an institutionalist lens provides a vocabulary and framework to account for the professions' agency and their broader societal role. While this social role is hinted at in previous work (e.g. Abbott, 1988), research informed by institutional theory gives greater prominence to the idea that professions both influence and are influenced by an ecology of surrounding institutions (Suddaby & Muzio, 2015).

2.6 Theories of Professional Organizations

These three lenses can also be applied to theories relating to professional organizations. We explore this now, confining our discussion to (heteronomous and autonomous) organizations that employ professionals and saving the discussion of professional membership associations for Section 4.

2.6.1 Functionalist Perspectives on Professional Organizations

Although functionalism has been somewhat discredited as a theory for understanding professions as an occupational category (see Section 2.1), it remains influential to research on professional organizations, even if this is not always explicitly acknowledged (Hinings, 2005). Much of this work also draws on contingency theory to classify 'professional organizations' as a distinct ideal-type that is functional under certain conditions.

The starting point for this literature is what Gunz and Gunz (2006) term the 'organizational-professional-conflict'. According to Blau and Scott (1962: 60–4), core professional values – autonomy, commitment to service and expert knowledge – are incompatible with the ideal-typical bureaucratic values of discipline and rule compliance. This literature also assumes that professionals have a weaker psychological contract with organizations. Whereas bureaucrats (as 'locals') are committed to the organization that employs them, professionals (sometimes as private contractors) are more mobile, have looser ties to organizations and have stronger 'cosmopolitan' orientations (Gouldner, 1957; Raelin, 1991). As such, a guiding assumption is that 'professionals should not fit well within formal organizations, because the essence of professionalism is autonomy and that of organization is control' (Gunz & Gunz, 2006: 259). Table 4 provides a typical summary of these tensions in relation to the 'social values' of professionals and managers.

Table 4 The Social Values of Managers and
Professionals

Managers	Professionals
Hierarchy	Participation
Respect for authority	Defiance of authority
Corporate efficiency	Social justice
Team player	Individual initiative
Career	Quality of life

Source: Raelin (1991)

A related strand of research within the functionalist tradition focuses on the specific characteristics of 'professional' organizations (Powell et al., 1999). Perhaps the most influential statement of this is Henry Mintzberg's (1979) ideal type of 'professional bureaucracy'. According to Mintzberg (1979), like the classic machine-model of bureaucracy, professional organizations (autonomous and heteronomous) provide highly standardized services such as predictable forms of treatment, teaching, or accounting advice. However, given their complexity, coordination and control is not achieved through formal rules and direct supervision but through the standardization of knowledge, skills and competences acquired through external education and socialization. Professionals are required to exercise discretion, applying knowledge on a case-by-case basis (what Mintzberg describes as 'pigeonholing'). One consequence of this arrangement is that, in a professional bureaucracy, effective decision-making power rests with members of the operating core, i.e. those who contribute directly towards the production of the company's core products and services (such as doctors in a hospital or academics in a university).

Another influential theory influenced by the functionalist lens is Greenwood et al.'s (1990) notion of the P2 archetype (or partnership model), developed with reference to large accounting and law firms (also see Greenwood & Hinings, 1993; Cooper et al., 1996) but applied more widely (e.g. public sector) (see Kirkpatrick & Ackroyd, 2003). This approach extends the work of Mintzberg (1979) by suggesting that, in a P2 archetype, organizational structures and systems also 'consistently embody a single interpretative scheme' (Greenwood & Hinings, 1993: 1055). Interpretative schemes refer to the distinctive set of values and beliefs and purposes that shape 'what an organization should be doing, of how it should be doing it and how it should be judged' (Greenwood & Hinings, 1988: 295). In the case of the P2, this scheme emphasizes the values of professionalism and partnership (Greenwood et al., 1990; Cooper et al., 1996) (explaining why the 'P' is squared).

More recently, others have developed these ideas to theorize variations in form *between* professional organizations. Von Nordenflycht (2010), for example, distinguishes between PSFs operating across a wide range of business and non-business sectors. All PSFs, he argues, have three distinctive characteristics: knowledge intensity, low capital intensity and a professionalized workforce. However, these characteristics vary between organizational settings, leading to a taxonomy of four main types of PSFs, including: *Classic PSFs* (law and accounting) and *Professionalized campuses* (hospitals), but also *Neo-PSFs* (such as consulting firms) and *Technology Developers* (R&D labs) which lack an externally professionalized workforce.

2.6.2 Professional Organizations through the Power and Institution Lens

In contrast to the large body of functionalist perspectives on professional organizations, researchers adopting the power and institutional lens have been less concerned with the organizational dimension. This is partly explained by the historic divisions between sociology of occupations and sociology of organizations noted earlier. Recently, though, attention has focused on how the occupational and organizational dimensions can be combined in dynamic ways (Muzio & Kirkpatrick, 2011). This has led to an emerging strand of research that draws on ideas from both the power lens (especially the notion of professional projects) and institutional theory to address *two* related concerns. First is how professional claims in the wider occupational domain translate in terms of influence and practices within organizations. Second is the reverse case of how the strategies of organizations may also influence the nature and trajectory of professionalization projects.

2.6.3 Professional Agency in Shaping Formal Organization and Management Practice

The connection between professional power in the labour market arena and the ability to control or influence practice in organizations is well understood within the sociology of professions (Barley & Tolbert, 1991). An early example is Freidson's (1988) classic account of the profession of medicine and its effective dominance over healthcare institutions. Freidson notes that, while the medical profession relies on the hospital as an organization setting, in many respects the hospital is also an 'appendage of clinical practice' in that 'hospital policies and procedures are controlled by the physicians who use it as a place in which to bed and treat their patients' (1988: 111). This idea that professional agendas might overlap with (and capture) organizational practices is also central to Ackroyd's

(1996) notion of 'double closure'. Ackroyd argues that professions 'maintain considerable control by combining a closure in the labour market outside employing organizations through their associations and the practice of licensing practitioners, but they also maintain control inside employing organizations as well, through informal organization (1996: 600). The most successful professions, he contends, 'occupy specific, and often strategically powerful enclaves within large organizations' which, in turn gives the ability to shape and determine the strategies of those organizations (601).

These insights draw attention to how powerful elites within the professions might exploit organizations to expand their privileges at the expense of subordinate groups (Hanlon, 1998). For example, drawing on labour process theory, Ackroyd and Muzio (2007) have shown how senior partners in law firms sought to expand the proportion of salaried fee earners (who generate most of the revenue) in relation to profit-sharing partners. Such strategies, they note, have an impact on working conditions, driving a wedge between a shrinking elite of powerful partners who realize a disproportionate share of the rewards of professional status and an expanding cohort of rank-and-file workers exposed to work intensification and decreasing levels of autonomy. There is also a strong gendered dimension at play, as partners are predominantly male whilst salaried associates are predominantly female (Tomlinson et al., 2013) (also see Section 6.3.2).

More recently, scholars working within both the power and institutional lenses have raised critical concerns about how far professional status always does translate into organizational influence (Fayard et al., 2017; Sandholtz et al., 2019; Huising, 2015; Wright et al., 2017). Focusing on HR managers, Chung et al. (2019) note how jurisdictional claims associated with upward mobility are often substantially watered down within organizations as professionals struggle for credibility. Similarly, Huising (2015) considers how professionals that have achieved degrees of labour market closure, such as university laboratory technicians, enact authority within organizations to secure compliance from their clients (including managers and other professionals). Interestingly, she notes that the most successful professionals are those who secure legitimacy and 'relational authority' by engaging in routine, low-skill 'scut work'. By contrast, others have drawn on the concept of institutional work to explore how professions struggle to enact core values and associated practices within organizations (Currie et al., 2012; Micelotta & Washington, 2013). Wright et al. (2017), for example, explore how Australian physicians engage in 'institutional maintenance work' to uphold their professional values of service and altruisms against the demands of organizational rationalization.

2.6.4 Organizations as Agents of Professionalization

While professionals may have an emerging role in shaping organizational structures and practices, it is also possible that this is a two-way relationship. This idea, of course, is not new. As we saw, there is a considerable body of literature focusing on how encroaching forms of management and technology in organizations are leading to de- professionalization (see also Sections 3 and 6). Indeed, it is suggested that there has been a 'dramatic rise in organizational dominance ... to the point that many professionals now ply their trade almost exclusively within complex organizations' (Chung et al., 2019: 36). However, while organizations affect *individual* autonomy, they may also have wider consequences for professional projects in the labour market arena.

This relationship between organizations and professionalization projects is suggested by several diffuse strands in the literature. One of the best-cited examples is Freidson's account of professional re-stratification (1994). Central to this account is the idea that, in response to pressures for tighter financial and management control within organizations, professions such as medicine, accounting and engineering are reorganizing themselves along functional lines as a defensive strategy. This process, Freidson argues, has led to the emergence of 'knowledge elites' and 'administrative elites' within the professions. The former comprises professionals involved in research and education, helping to create new standards and regulations. By contrast, 'administrative elites' comprise professionals taking on formal management roles and responsibility for the coordination and direction of rank and file practitioners. Freidson therefore highlights the way in which organizational restructuring has triggered changes in the wider dynamics of professionalization and how these unfold both within and beyond organizations.

Institutional theorists have also explored the wider role of corporations in sponsoring emergent professionalization projects. According to Suddaby and Muzio (2015: 36), it is important to 'view the relationship between professions and other related institutions as an institutional ecology in which professionalization projects, if they are to succeed, must ally with a related institution or institutions' (2015: 36). In this regard, large corporations, including PSFs have been key actors (David et al., 2013). Classic professions such as law and architecture have increasingly reoriented their allegiances from the nation state to the market and the large corporation. Examples of this include the recognition of alternative qualification pathways initiated by firms (Malhotra et al., 2006) and the legitimization of new organizational forms such as multidisciplinary practices (Greenwood & Suddaby, 2006). In the case of emerging professions, such as management consulting and project management, it is also noted how the active participation of PSFs in the running of professional associations has led to a departure from the goals of occupational closure in favour of alternative strategies that align more closely with corporate (or employer) interests (Hodgson, Paton & Muzio, 2015; Kirkpatrick et al., 2019).

Taken together, these strands suggest a need to 'revisit theories of professionalism, which did not fully anticipate the shift of professional work to the context of large organizations' (Suddaby et al., 2007: 25). We will return to this idea later on, as we examine the role of membership of associations and regulatory agencies in shaping professionalization projects in Section 4 and the changing dynamics of professional organizations in Section 5.

3 The Demise of the Professions?

3.1 Introduction

The idea that professionalism is somehow in terminal decline has been a feature of many seminal accounts of the professions and remains influential (Reed, 2007). Brint (1994), for example, concluded that by the late 1960s the 'golden age' of professionals had already passed, while the title of Krause's (1996) history of professions in five countries (United Kingdom, USA, Germany, Italy, France), *The Death of the Guilds*, is largely self-explanatory. Implied by these grand narratives is the idea that professions – even those most established – have lost ground, and that public trust in their capacity to self-regulate has waned (Adams, 2017). According to Ackroyd (2016: 27–8), 'Whatever theoretical view is taken, it is difficult to conclude that professions are as important as they were even a few decades ago.'

This chapter reviews the current arguments surrounding this hypothesis, focusing on *three* challenges: cultural de-legitimization; a technological revolution rendering professional work obsolete; and new political priorities and re-regulatory agendas. Taken together, these challenges are assumed to result in de-professionalization, meaning the loss of *collective* and *individual* professional autonomy (Freidson, 1994). The former concerns professional associations' reduced power to regulate access to labour markets, whilst the latter – consistent with the predictions of Marxist theory – highlights the reduced autonomy of practitioners within the workplace. However, while these predictions of decline and decay are commonplace in the literature, as we shall see, they are also widely challenged.

3.2 Cultural Delegitimization and the Loss of Confidence in Expertise

The legitimacy of the professions is dependent on their cultural authority, a theme emphasized by the functionalist, power and institutional lenses discussed so far. Historically, there is evidence that more established, 'collegiate' professions experienced a high level of public trust. Survey data going back to the 1980s indicates how professionals such as doctors, teachers and judges are consistently viewed as trustworthy by over 80 per cent of respondents (Ipsos MORI – see Box 1). However, despite these trends, several scholars in the 1970s began to warn against the risk posed by experts. Lieberman (1970), for instance, devoted an entire book designed to expose the 'tyranny of experts', while Brint (1994: 16) asserted that the critics of professionalism had 'correctly argued ... [that] undisputed claims to representing "the public good" can lead to excesses of self-interest legitimated in the name of professional autonomy'.

Possibly one of the most-cited critics of professionalism is the Austrian philosopher and Roman Catholic priest – Ivan Illich (1976; 1977) – who wrote about the over-reliance on professional expertise in everyday life. According to Illich, experts such as doctors, lawyers and teachers have a disabling effect because they substitute for common-sense solutions to problems which may be more legitimate, practical and even efficient. Indeed, Illich develops the concept of counter-productivity whereby the professions contribute to the very same problems they are designed to address. Hence, doctors might perpetuate ill health, while teachers might increase the ignorance of students and so on. All of this, Illich argues, generates a cost for individuals who lose the ability to solve their own problems and become overly dependent on technocratic elites.

More recently, concerns about the so-called 'tyranny of experts' (Chafetz, 1994) have morphed into a wider process of cultural demystification, with potentially serious implications for the professions. According to Leicht (2016), this results from the 'deadly embrace' of neo-liberalism as an economic ideology and postmodernism as a cultural tendency. These usually unrelated forces, he argues, have come together to create a hostile environment for professionals, their work and organizations. The first, neo-liberalism is a well-understood development (see also Reed, 1996; Hanlon, 1998). Essentially, it celebrates the supremacy of markets (Stiglitz, 2013) and is suspicious of any institution, such as professions, which may interfere with their operation. Indeed, as alternatives to markets, the professions (and state-owned bureaucracies) are condemned both on functional (as less efficient) and ethical (as they favour producers over consumers or taxpayers) grounds. Conversely, a postmodern critique of professions draws on some of the original arguments developed by Illich. From this perspective, professional expertise quashes diversity, democracy and individual self-reliance whilst reproducing the interest and world views of dominant elites. Although originating from very different theoretical and political standpoints, neo-liberal and postmodernist critiques coalesce into a shared narrative of individual choice and of hostility to the assumed self-interest of the professions.

Similar themes are developed in Nichol's recent book, *The Death of Expertise* (2017). For Nichols, political events such as Brexit (in the United Kingdom) and the election of Trump (in the USA) are indicative of the marginalization of professions and decreasing levels of public trust in their judgement. Nichols attributes this to a number of factors. One is the massification and commercialization of university education, which produces increasingly bland programmes and safe spaces where graduates are not pushed to develop critical thinking. Armed with credentials and an inflated sense of their abilities, the educated public is much more ready to query and dismiss professional advice without really understanding its foundations. As discussed in Section 3.3, the distance between expert and layperson is further reduced by developments in information technology and social media. With the erosion of editorial control, the internet has led to a proliferation of poor, if not fraudulent, sources, which drown out more legitimate ones. This has led to a world that, according to Michael Gove, 'has had enough of experts' and no longer values their role or accepts their authority.

Even more significant is the increasing number of well-publicized instances of professional failure. We use the term 'failure' here to include cases of culpability (including negligence and more active forms of misconduct) as well as more ordinary cases where professionals simply got it wrong. Examples of the latter include shifting medical advice (such as on smoking, drinking or even egg consumption), medicines with serious side effects (Thalidomide), and failure to accurately forecast elections or predict economic recessions (as in the 2007 financial crisis), as well as seemingly flawed economic forecasts. These 'failures' reflect many issues, including the public's misunderstanding of the nature of science and of the limits of expertise, as well as the inherent difficulty, unpredictability, or 'wicked' nature of the problems that professionals must address. However, whatever the causes, the net result is a tendency to discount all professional expertise as confirmation biases encourage a sceptical public to remember only the occasions where professionals 'got it wrong'.

Much more corrosive of public trust are cases where professionals and professional firms are involved in unethical or even illegal behaviour (Muzio et al., 2016; Currie et al., 2019). Most obvious are cases of rogue individuals, such as Harold Shipman in the English NHS, who flaunt the deontological codes of professions, abusing their position of trust to engage in criminal activities (Kershaw & Moorhead, 2013). These 'bad apples' delegitimize the entire

Box 1 Have We Had Enough of Experts?

The UK Ipsos MORI Veracity Index annually assesses which roles are most trusted by the public. Despite Michael Gove's (then Justice Secretary) notorious attack on experts, the professions consistently rank as the 'most trusted' occupations, with public confidence (consistently) highest in nurses, doctors, teachers, scientists and professors. And, although scores for the legal profession are much lower, it is trusted far more than banking, politics and journalism. Thus, it seems like the British public has not had enough of experts after all.

Polls conducted in other countries also find professionals to be the most trusted groups in society with confidence in nurses, like the United Kingdom, the highest of all in the USA, Canada and Australia (McCarthy, 2018; Insights West, 2017; Roy Morgan 2017).

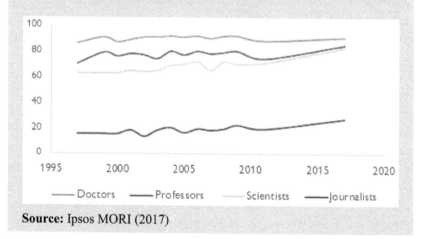

Source: Ipsos MORI (2017)

profession because they undermine trust in professional socialization and regulation regimes and contradict traditional claims of professional integrity. More problematically, numerous corporate scandals such as Enron (Grey, 2003; Coffee, 2006), Parmalat (Gabbioneta et al., 2013), Lehman Brothers (Kershaw & Moorhead, 2013) and the Panama Papers debacle (Ježek and Jeppe, 2017; Trautman, 2017), to name a few, illustrate how professionals and professional firms facilitated the very sort of corporate wrongdoing they were supposed to prevent (see Boxes 2 and 3 for examples). These cases highlight a series of structural flaws, such as conflict of interest (Gabbioneta et al., 2014) or client capture (Dinovitzer et al., 2014) which make professional organizations particularly prone to fail in their role as gatekeepers (Coffee, 2006) and to engage in systematic wrongdoing (Sikka & Willmott, 2013).

Thus, the result of these developments is a new environment where both the mystique and authority of the professions are eroded, as their claims are dismissed, their motives doubted and their services treated as mere commodities.

3.3 The Disruptive Potential of New Technology

A further source of perceived threat to the professions originates from advances in technology. This idea, of course, is not new and was already anticipated in the 1970s (see for example, the power lens discussed in Section 2). At that time, the explosion of scientific and technological knowledge led to very different scenarios. Whilst for some it signalled the advent of a post-industrial society (Bell, 1973), for others it was evidence of an impending 'de-professionalization' (Haug, 1972) or 'proletarianization' (Oppenheimer, 1972). Haug (1972), for example, argued that developments in computing technology were facilitating the codification of professional knowledge, simultaneously increasing its accessibility to non-professionals whilst eroding one of the key qualities demarcating

BOX 2 PARMALAT: THE COLLAPSE OF AN ITALIAN DYNASTY

Parmalat, a large, multinational Italian dairy and food corporation, practised one of the largest corporate financial frauds of the decade before it filed for bankruptcy in 2003, leaving behind a 'hole' of 14 billion euros – a sum almost twice the company's 2002 sales turnover. Investigations revealed that the company's reported financial condition had long been falsified and misrepresented during the thirteen years it was listed on *Borsa Italiana* (the Milan Stock Exchange). Yet, the professional gatekeepers (auditors, analysts, lawyers and others), whom the market has long trusted to filter, verify and assess complicated financial information, failed in their fiduciary duty (Coffee, 2006). Securities analysts, for instance, consistently issued positive recommendations and over 85 per cent of their equity research reports recommended buying or holding the company's shares. Likewise, bond rating firm Standard & Poor's maintained an investment-grade rating up to ten days before Parmalat sought bankruptcy protection. And it was only in 2003, when the Italian Professional Accounting Association declared that auditors would be held responsible for the accounts of subsidiary companies in a group, that Deloitte & Touche – one of Parmalat's two auditors – issued a 'disclaimer' on the company's financial accounts, as it could not determine the value of investments in an offshore private equity fund.

> ### Box 3 Enron's Collapse and the Failure of Professional Ethics
>
> In one of the largest bankruptcies in US history, in which investors were left $15 billion in debt and 20,000 workers found themselves without a job in December 2001, gatekeeping professionals not only failed to expose Enron's fraudulent financial statements (Gabbioneta et al., 2014), but many were actively involved in the gigantic corruption that ensued. Enron's auditor, Arthur Andersen, for example, was accused of a whole host of issues, including helping create accounting techniques that enabled corporate fraud to be perpetrated. Nine prestigious financial institutions were named as key players in a series of fraudulent transactions that ultimately cost shareholders more than $25 billion. Two law firms were accused of 'malpractice' because they failed to respond to red flags about Enron's accounting practices (Gabbioneta et al., 2014). Moreover, all fifteen of the of the company's financial analysts who made recommendations on Enron's shares rated these as worthy of buying right up to the point of bankruptcy. As the architect of many of Enron's corporate strategies and in close contact with a client heading for the abyss, the world's pre-eminent consulting firm – McKinsey – apparently foresaw nothing wrong and issued no cautionary advice (Fincham & Clark, 2002). Instead, it endorsed Enron's strategic repositioning and praised its 'asset light' strategy (Kipping et al., 2006).

the professions from other groups – mastery over an exclusive body of knowledge.

More recently, predictions about the 'technology threat' to professions have acquired a new lease of life. Advances in robotics, artificial intelligence and machine learning are thought to be ushering in a 'Second Machine Age' (Brynjolfsson & McAfee, 2014) or 'a fourth industrial revolution' (Schwab, 2016), which, this time, will affect knowledge-based activities as well as manual ones. Indeed, there are widespread predictions of how new technologies will disrupt even traditional professions, such as medicine (Harz, 2017). *Fortune* magazine for example, asserts that 'Technology will replace 80% of what doctors do' (Khosla, 2012), whilst two leading futurologists predict that the advent of intelligent machines will eventually render the professions obsolete (Susskind & Susskind, 2015).

This latest contention that traditional forms of professional expertise are being fundamentally disrupted by technology rests upon the assessment that new technologies are profoundly different from those of the past (Kaplan,

2015). The key difference relates to 'Moore's Law', the continuous increase in the power of computing hardware, software, connectivity, networking speed and data storage, enabling smart machines to perform progressively more complex tasks. Hence, commentators such as Susskind and Susskind (2015) argue that new technologies are a uniquely disruptive force without historical precedent, impacting both low- and highly skilled occupations (Wajcman, 2017). Examples of the use of robots in professional services, such as substituting for a pharmacist in dispensing prescriptions, demonstrate how professional work is not immune to automation. As predicted some time ago by Zuboff (1988), professional monopolies may be finally dismantled through the substitution of professional labour by expert systems.

Somewhat less radically, the uptake of new technological solutions has enabled PSFs to automate and routinize labour-intensive tasks such as due diligence in law or auditing in accountancy. Additionally, leading PSFs such as law firm Simmons & Simmons and consultancy firm McKinsey's are deploying Web-based technology to develop new marketing channels such as subscription-based services (Smets et al., 2017). However, new technological solutions transcend traditional PSFs. Often predicated on new business models, new entrants such as Axiom and Riverview Law are pioneering new services and ways of working that are disrupting traditional practices. For instance, the development of platform technology is facilitating the development of virtual forms of organizing where individual practitioners and firms may come together in fluid and flexible ways to discharge particular projects or transactions. Alongside networked organizations, new technologies are enabling small numbers of expert professionals to use artificial intelligence to service relationship patterns in mass markets (Broschak, 2015). Traditionally professional services have not been at the forefront of organizational innovation but have operated on the basis of established models or imported these from other sectors such as manufacturing or public administration; yet the increasing possibilities of information technology and growing pressures towards innovation and efficiency in the service sector (Susskind & Susskind, 2015) may mean that in the future new organizational models and forms will increasingly originate from this sector.

New technologies also have the potential to empower users to understand and evaluate professional expertise. As Web-based solutions and intelligent machines become more sophisticated and accessible, professionals can no longer assume the old asymmetry of knowledge between themselves and users (McGinnis & Pearce, 2014). An example of this is disintermediation platforms that allow users to access expertise without the mediation of the professions (Susskind & Susskind, 2015). Thus, 'crowdsourcing' solutions such as MedHelp, PatientsLikeMe and HealthUnlocked guide users to answers, bypassing professional channels. Using social networking technologies, internet communities potentially empower non-experts to generate shared bodies of experience and disseminate this knowledge in ways that were previously unimaginable (Campbell, 2016).

Other examples of user empowerment are digital health services, which (theoretically at least) allow users to collect large volumes of data and 'analyse it with a sophistication that rivals many clinicians' (Susskind & Susskind, 2015: 51). For some commentators, 'self-generated data by smart, hyper connected patients' could ultimately 'represent a serious challenge to medical paternalism' (Topol, 2015: 12). The traditional top-down power structure with 'doctor knowing best' is transformed as 'the patient becomes the chief operating officer', turning to the doctor only when 'it's particularly important' (Topol, 2015: 12). In the longer term, according to Susskind and Susskind (2015), technology will promote the democratization of professional expertise, making it more difficult for professionals to retain not only established practices but also the basis of their legitimacy and authority (see Section 3.1).

Hence, the literature in this area stresses two related challenges. Firstly, professionals will increasingly be substituted by technologies, capable of being operated by lesser skilled forms of labour or even by consumers themselves. Secondly, technology will make professional expertise more transparent and accountable, allowing consumers and employers to challenge, control and assess expertise. Yet, while these grand narratives are often influential with policymakers, their predications are rarely tested. Those studies that do focus on professional settings also suggest that the 'disruptive' impact is far 'less than the headlines would have us believe' (Remus & Levey 2016). Drawing on hours billed, Remus and Levey (2016) identified thirteen broad categories of work undertaken by lawyers and then assessed the probability of each being automated. They conclude that, since most of the work is 'unstructured', only 13 per cent of all legal work is (currently) capable of being automated.

3.4 New Political Priorities and Changing Regulation

As we saw in Section 2, the power lens emphasizes how the success of professional projects is, to some extent, contingent upon state support to sanction labour market closure (Timmermans, 2008). This may assume various forms, including voluntary certification, Royal Charters (in the United Kingdom) and state licencing (Kleiner, 2013).

However, while these forms of state-sanctioned monopoly are quite common in developed countries, from the 1970s the legitimacy of professional self-governance came under sustained attack (Muzio & Ackroyd, 2005; Leicht & Lyman, 2006). Indeed, over the last thirty years or so, the professions in most national contexts have been exposed to forms of re-regulation (Quack & Schüßler, 2015). For some commentators, the scale of reform has been so extensive that the professions' powers of self-regulation are now 'virtually non-existent' (Adams, 2017: 70). In what follows, we review these arguments and raise questions about the nature and extent of regulatory change (this topic will also be explored in Section 4).

The 1980s saw the rise of a neo-liberal political agenda within Anglo-Saxon countries, which emphasized the 'invisible hand' of free markets as the basis of economic progress and social policy solutions (Leicht & Lyman, 2006). Whereas the professions had traditionally been viewed as key stakeholders in Fordist social compacts (Reed, 1996; Hanlon, 1998), the new right agenda portrayed them as rent-seeking economic agents who used self-regulatory privileges to further their own interests (Philipsen, 2009). A notable example is 'private interest theory', which takes the view that the self-regulation of professional markets restricts competition and enables professions to earn economic rents (Stephen, 2013). In the words of British Prime Minister Margaret Thatcher, the professions were 'little republics' unaccountable to public scrutiny (Burrage, 1997).

This ideological hostility was strengthened by a series of national and transnational investigations examining the effects of professional self-regulation, all of which concluded that statutory market protections and other practices were anti-competitive, unnecessary to safeguard the public interest and, ultimately, 'serve[d] mainly the private interests of the profession' (OECD, 2007: 9). Rejecting the premise that professional services are unique, bodies such as the British Office of Fair Trading (2001) and Australian Trade Practices Commission (1993) recommended that market privileges should be removed and that professional services should be regulated just like any other industry. In a popular expression at the time, acquiring professional services should be no different from buying a can of baked beans.

In the USA, a similar critique has been made of occupational licensing (Kleiner & Krueger, 2013. According to Young (2002), licensing 'has limited consumer choice, raised consumer costs, increased practitioner income, limited practitioner mobility, and deprived the poor of adequate services – all without demonstrated improvements in the quality or safety of the licensed activities'. Decisions about when and who to license, he suggests, are frequently made with little input from the public and sometimes with only limited (or no) evidence of likely benefits to consumers. All this raises unnecessary costs for consumers (who may pay higher prices for licensed expertise) and taxpayers who foot the bill for increased state regulation (Thornton & Timmons, 2015). These concerns have been further exaggerated by studies of the economic consequences of legalized occupational closure (Kleiner & Krueger, 2013). Kleiner (2013), for example, finds that while licensing is associated with a 15–18 per cent wage premium for occupations, overall its impact on service quality for consumers is negative or, at best, insignificant.

These challenges have led to adjustments to the 'regulative bargain' between professions and the state, although these have taken multiple forms. On the one hand, there has been a drive to remove perceived barriers to competition and the operation of free markets for expert (professional) services. On the other, there have been moves to *extend* state involvement in the regulation of the professions. Either way, the assumed direction of travel has been to limit the power and autonomy of professions to regulate themselves.

3.4.1 Enhancing Competition

From the late 1980s onwards, the professions and their organizations (notably PSFs) became the target of several types of re-regulatory measures aimed at increasing competition (Philipsen, 2009; Stephen, 2013). In Europe, this can be seen with initiatives such as the 2013 Professional Qualification Directive which aims to facilitate the mobility of qualified professionals within the internal market (Canton et al., 2014). In the USA, growing political and public concerns about occupational licensing (see Section 3.4) also led to calls for a different approach (Vaheesan & Pasquale, 2018). Young (2002) refers to 'sunset laws' which, in some states, now require public agencies (including licensing boards) to justify their existence. Kleiner (2013) notes that while in the past most challenges to licensing emerged from the courts over the enforcement of antitrust laws, there is now an increasing tendency for state legislators to propose less costly alternatives to licensing, such as voluntary certification.

In the case of PSFs, the watering down of 'conduct and 'entity' regulations has also intensified competition. With regard to 'conduct', virtually all Anglo-Saxon jurisdictions have now eliminated restrictions relating to advertising or mandatory/recommended fee schedules for PSFs. Such reforms, whilst pioneered in the USA (Adams, 2017) and the United Kingdom and Australia, rapidly spread to other countries including Italy (Micelotta & Washington, 2013), France, Finland and Germany (Stephen, 2013). At the transnational level, the European Union's 2009 Professional Services Competition Initiative also recommended the abolition of restrictive practices in five professions across twenty-five countries (Terry 2009).

Turning to 'entity' regulations, until the 1990s it was illegal for PSFs to adopt an organizational form other than a 'professional partnership'. As a consequence, firms were not allowed to form companies or multi-disciplinary businesses or to incorporate and become listed on the stock exchange. However, these restrictions have now been relaxed or removed in many countries. For example, audit firms were permitted to operate as limited liability partnerships, initially in the USA from the early 1990s and elsewhere thereafter (Bush et al., 2007). Restrictions relating to the ownership of legal practices were first removed in Australia (Parker, 2008) and then in England and Wales (Flood, 2012), allowing law firms to raise capital from external investors and even list on the stock exchange.

3.4.2 State Involvement

While these developments might suggest a drift towards a more laissez-faire relationship between the state and professions – lowering restrictions on competition – in other domains the direction of travel has been towards *greater* state involvement in the internal affairs of professions to curtail their self-regulatory powers (Adams, 2017). Evetts (2002: 347) describes this as a process of 'acquired regulation', a 'form of externally required, but internally devised and operated, regulation' (by professions) linked to 'external monitoring, assessment and audit'. While acquired regulation is not new – especially in the case of 'state mediated' (Johnson, 1972) professions – in recent years it has been extended. In the case of law, for example, there have been moves to separate the representative and regulatory functions of professional bodies. The Legal Services Act 2007 (LSA) removed the self-governing powers of professional bodies in England and Wales and 'implemented a regulatory model and structures more closely tied to government' (Paton, 2010: 2236). Increasingly, professional bodies such as the Law Society (solicitors' profession) and General Council of the Bar (barristers) no longer exercise direct responsibility for regulating members.

A related development moves towards more intrusive external audit and monitoring of the work of professions (Verbeeten & Speklé, 2015). In the public sector, for instance, performance management has assumed a variety of approaches, including 'Transparent Public Ranking' (TPR), whereby the results of particular agencies (schools, hospitals, universities) are measured against a set of centrally determined performance indicators, published as league tables. The TPR model – sometimes referred to as 'targets and terror' (Bevan & Hood, 2006) – was premised on the assumption that providers respond to threats to their reputation by trying to improve their performance.

Hence, overall, it seems that the professions in many countries now operate within a regulatory landscape different to that which existed only a few decades ago (Quack & Schüßler, 2015; Adams, 2017). Self-regulation is under attack as governments (and transnational bodies) unbundle the regulative from representative functions of professional associations and challenge what they perceive to be restrictive practices. However, the impact of these forms of re-regulation on the ability of professionals to control their primary fields of operation is sometimes overstated. To explore this question further, we turn to the macro level of analysis, focusing on the changing ability of professions to control and regulate occupations.

4 Professional Occupations

4.1 Introduction

This is the first of three sections examining contemporary developments in the professions at three distinct levels of analysis: macro, meso and micro. We begin at the macro level by focusing on the occupational dimension. Specifically, we look at changes to how the professions are organized collectively and to the role and functions of the professional associations that represent and coordinate professionals (Greenwood et al., 2002). Drawing on the ideas reviewed in Section 2, we argue that professional associations' principal focus of attention is directed at 'projects' aimed at controlling jurisdictions *and* the wider formation of institutions. However, a key question is how successful these attempts to achieve occupational control have been, especially following the neo-liberal critiques of professional monopoly described in Section 3. Here we review these debates and consider the evidence base relating to current levels of professional organization and occupational closure in the USA and (to a lesser extent) the United Kingdom.

4.2 The Organizations of Professions

As we have seen, central to all theories of professions is the idea that, as collective agents, they seek to establish degrees of control and closure over particular jurisdictions or labour markets. Because achieving such control necessitates 'deliberate action by an occupation' (Millerson, 1964: 9), this inevitably directs our attention to the role of professions' formal membership organizations (Adler et al., 2008; Greenwood et al., 2002). Indeed, it is partly for this reason that many accounts simply accept Reader's (1966: 163) view: 'An occupation's rise to professional standing can be pretty accurately charted by reference to the progress of its professional institute or association.'

These assertions do not mean that professional associations always fully represent the occupational communities they claim to work for. Research shows that professional associations can be highly conservative bodies, often captured by elite groups of practitioners committed to defending the status quo (Van Wijk et al., 2013; Greenwood et al., 2002). This may generate a classic tension in associations, which are 'democratic in form and oligarchic in operation' (Rego & Vardana, 2009: 1253). Similarly, membership of associations is highly variable and in some cases represents only a fraction of a given target occupation (PARN, 2015). Often, rank-and-file practitioners are unaware of and uninterested in the associations that claim to represent them (Chan & Anteby, 2015). However, these caveats do not fundamentally alter the critical role that associations play as key agents of professionalization.

4.2.1 Membership-Based Organizations

Organizations advancing professional interests are best understood as 'membership-based organizations' (MBO). Typically non-profit, MBOs 'promote and protect' the 'mutual interests' of 'individuals or organizations from a specific domain that voluntarily join together' (Hudson, 2013: 4). They determine membership requirements and charge fees (sometimes the primary source of income). Traditionally, national organizations established local chapters with voting rights, leading to a federated style of decision-making. The common practice was for a small group to assume management responsibility for their respective chapters, often on a voluntary basis and outside of work hours, although the current trend is towards employing professional managers to administer association activities (Hwang & Powell, 2009).

This latter trend has led to an increasing polarization between associations in terms of the coordination and economic governance functions they provide to members. Useful for understanding this is Spillman's (2012; 2018) distinction between 'dinner-club' associations, 'service' associations and 'policy-shaping' associations (cf. Spillman, 2012, 90–2). Following Galambos (1965), Spillman notes how 'dinner clubs' tend to have weak formal organization and identity but may 'occupy a useful niche when more informal networks between similar businesses are difficult to sustain' (2018: 19). By contrast, 'service' associations tend to be 'more proactive in sustaining long-term systemic programmes and typically involve more differentiated organization and leadership' (90–1).

4.2.2 Professional Associations

As noted, professional associations represent a particular sub-category of MBOs. Like MBOs, they often have long histories and face similar governance

Table 5 Primary and Secondary Functions of Professional Associations

Primary Functions	Secondary Functions
Increasing membership; Qualifying members (certification); Registering qualified members; Research and knowledge exchange; Preserving high standards of conduct.	Raising professional status; Lobbying and advocating on behalf of members; Providing opportunities for networking and social activities; Provision of member services, including welfare benefits.

Source: Millerson (1964)

challenges. However, it is also necessary to highlight distinctions between 'professional associations'. According to Millerson (1964), the term encompasses 'any association, which directly aims at the improvement of any aspect of professional practice: for example, by providing a qualification, by controlling conduct, by coordinating technical information, by pressing for better conditions of employment' (32–3). Millerson (1964) differentiates between primary and secondary functions of associations (see Table 5) and further distinguishes between four types: 'prestige associations'; 'study associations'; 'occupational associations' and 'qualifying associations'.

Of these four types, the latter – qualifying associations – are the most developed and correspond to the stereotypical image of a professional association. By contrast, *prestige associations* seek to attract members based on some measure of publicly recognized distinction. These might be exclusive (such as LeTip International), providing networks for business leads. Another type, *study associations* attract members interested in furthering knowledge or research in a particular field of study, for example the Royal Geographical Society in the United Kingdom or, in the USA, the Organization of American Historians. Lastly, an *occupational association* 'organizes professionals, without attempting to qualify them' (Millerson, 1964: 39).

While Millerson's (1964) taxonomy still offers a useful starting point for understanding the complex organizational landscape of contemporary professions, it is incomplete. According to Spillman (2012: 433), in recent years a discourse of 'professionalism' has also provided 'a pervasive vocabulary for American business associations'. These (trade) associations are assumed to have different objectives – representing organizations rather than individual practitioners – but many have become actively involved in certification. Indeed, Spillman (2012) reports that, in the USA, 24 per cent of associations had introduced 'standards and accreditation' while 40 per cent were involved in education and 'professional development'.

4.2.3 The Goals of Professional Associations

The aforementioned distinctions raise questions about the goals of different professional associations and whether they are all equally concerned with the objectives of occupational closure. As discussed in Section 2.3, professionalization is often viewed as a process of seeking labour market monopoly to further the economic interests and upward social mobility of aspiring occupations (Birket & Evans, 2005; Bol, 2014). For the most part, this assumption is supported by existing research. In the USA, both occupational licensing (Kleiner, 2013) and voluntary certification (Albert, 2017) are associated with significant wage premiums, especially in more established fields. Similarly, in the United Kingdom, Williams and Koumenta (2019: 18) conclude: 'jobs that have achieved higher levels of closure (i.e. more stringently licensed ones) have lower job insecurity, greater opportunities for skill-use, and higher continuous learning requirements'. Therefore, partly for this reason, the primary focus of many associations is on the development of certification, state licensing and 'legislated exclusivity' (Greenwood et al., 2002: 61).

However, the primacy of economic objectives should not be overstated. For some occupations, the objectives of occupational closure may be resented (or even resisted) on the grounds that it implies an increasing burden of regulation, with only marginal economic benefits (see Timmons (2010) on the experience of operating department practitioners in the English health service). It is also possible that labour market shelters that protect professions could 'thwart scientific and organizational innovation' and, in the longer term, limit a profession's ability to adapt to new challenges (Timmermans, 2008: 167).

Related to this, as we have seen, an inclusive definition of professional association suggests that the goal of pursuing labour market exclusivity is most advanced in so-called qualifying associations but may be less central to prestige or occupational associations. More broadly, the institutional lens (detailed in Section 2.4) suggests that professions have multiple objectives and functions (Suddaby & Viale, 2011: 423). As 'institutional agents', professions (and therefore their associations) have consequences for all three institutional pillars (see Section 2.4.3): regulative, normative and cognitive (Scott, 2008). Developing this idea, Spillman (2012: 246) argues that business/trade associations' 'professional strategies are more oriented to "claims-making in the market" than jurisdictional control'. The primary goal for these associations, she argues, is the 'production of cultural "infrastructure"' through networking and knowledge exchange. In this regard, associations can 'offer sustained resources for meaning-making about economic action – both strategic (articulating industry categories, networks, and fields) and expressive (collective identity, norms and status, and camaraderie)' (Spillman, 2018: 17).

4.3 The Professionalization of Occupations

Notwithstanding the aforementioned caveats concerning the goals of professional associations, an obvious question still regards their impact on emerging forms of professional regulation (or closure). As we saw in Section 3, neo-liberal economic ideologies have 'threatened the expert claims of professional groups' as 'an alternative to and protector of client and public welfare' (Leicht, 2016: 2). This hostile environment has also led others to suggest that many newer occupations – so-called knowledge workers – are predisposed towards strategies of 'marketization', using networks to acquire specialist forms of knowledge that have flexible niche market appeal (Reed, 1996). However, while accounts of long-term decline are influential, how accurate are they? To address this question, we consider three critical indicators of professionalization – the formation of associations, certification and state-sanctioned licensing (Weeden, 2002) – in the USA and, to a lesser extent, Europe. Drawing on secondary sources (Redbird, 2017; Kleiner, 2013) and earlier analysis conducted by ourselves (Kirkpatrick et al., 2017b), we show how, along all three dimensions, the evidence suggests that professionalization remains a robust institution with little sign of decay.

4.3.1 The Formation of Professional Associations

According to Lounsbury (2002: 256), in any jurisdiction the formation of associations 'is a useful indicator of professionalization efforts'. In recent times, these rates of formation have been especially pronounced. Estimates of the size of the population of professional associations vary greatly depending on the definition adopted. The US *Gale Encyclopedia* listed just over 6,700 'professional associations' in 2017, rising from 5,557 in 2004. By contrast, the government agency CareerOneStop recorded just under 2,500 associations operating nationally in the USA in 2016. Of these, 'qualifying associations' involved directly or indirectly in education and certification accounted for around a third. Across the total (CareerOneStop) association population, the largest number operate in healthcare and management sectors (Kirkpatrick et al., 2017) – see Table 6.

Although it is not possible to compare actual population shifts over time using this data, analysis of the foundation years of this current population of

Table 6 Professional Associations in the USA, by Type, 2016

	Number	%
Qualifying associations	711	31
Trade associations	645	28
Certification and training associations	334	14
Research networks, learned societies	328	14
Occupational membership associations	206	9
Government associations	42	2
Total	2,328	100

Source: Kirkpatrick et el., 2017

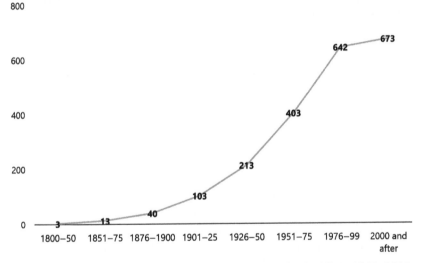

Figure 1 The Formation of Qualifying Associations in the USA, 1800–2015

associations revealed some interesting trends. Again drawing on Kirkpatrick et al. (2017), Figure 1 highlights variations over time in the rate of foundation of associations. Interestingly, the fastest rate of expansion was between 1976 and 1999, when 36 per cent of the current population was established. This period coincides with the high-water mark of neo-liberal influence in public policy (discussed in the previous section) and is contrary to Brint's (1994) assertion that the 1960s represented the 'golden age' of professional formation. By contrast, more recently, the rate of foundation has dipped to only 5 per cent of the current population, although, as we saw, figures from a different data source (the *Gale Encyclopedia*) suggest a continued upward trajectory.

These trends have coincided with changes in the functions and governance of associations. The former relate to the range of activities now in the purview of professional associations, including knowledge mobilization, education and certification (see Section 4.3.2) and, increasingly, taking on the role of quasi-regulatory agencies (Djelic and Sahlin-Andersson, 2006). Many associations act as 'paired organizations' (Lester, 2009), performing regulatory functions such as monitoring re-certification (Bartley, 2011) or assistance with the work of state licensing boards (Kleiner, 2013). In the United Kingdom, 32 per cent of professional associations have some kind of regulatory function (63 per cent for individuals and the remainder for individuals and organizations) (PARN, 2015).

This expansion has also been associated with a trend towards professionalizing the management and governance of membership-based organizations (Hudson, 2013). Broadly, this aligns with a move from 'dinner club' to 'service' associations described earlier (Spillman, 2012), weakening the role of volunteers in favour of full-time managers and executives. Hwang and Powell (2009: 270, 272) in their study of the non-profit sector describe this as a 'seismic shift towards organizational rationalization' potentially leading to new forms of 'professionalism' that are 'imbued with managerial aspirations and expectations'.

4.3.2 Certification

Voluntary certification schemes represent the second indicator of professionalization (Bartley, 2011). As explored in Section 2, certification is integral to most professionalization projects (Abbott, 1988) and may even be a precursor to state-sanctioned closure (Tolbert, 1996). Following an analysis of the NTPAUS directory, Kirkpatrick et al. (2017) observed a significant increase in certification programmes and that of organizations providing them. The former more than doubled (161 per cent increase) over an eight-year interval (2008–16). Likewise, the number of organizations providing certification rose by 124 per cent. The data also shows a drive to raise 'professional' standards by compulsory re-certification and third-party accreditation (Tschirhart et al., 2011).

Although driven primarily by professional associations, organizations (as employers) and practitioners have also fuelled demand for certification. This illustrates what Barley and Tolbert (1991) term the 'occupationalization' of organizations. Employers (including the state) may regard voluntary certification as a lower-cost way of increasing the supply and quality of expert human capital. From the perspective of individual practitioners, the possession of certification may enhance mobility and the prospect of so-called 'boundary-

Box 4 Professional Associations and International Certification: HRM
In today's world, professional associations are playing a key role in developing a 'certification ecosystem' both nationally and internationally (Bartley, 2011). For example, human resource (or personnel) managers, as an occupation, have struggled historically to gain professional recognition (Farndale & Brewster, 2005). However, more recently there are indications that this occupation is becoming increasingly professionalized through the advance of voluntary certification on a global scale. Focusing on the USA, the United Kingdom, Australia and Canada, Parks-Leduc et al. (2017) note how associations – such as the USA-based SHRM, with over 285,000 members in 165 countries, and the United Kingdom's Chartered Institute of Personnel and Development (CIPD), with over 140,000 members – have successfully embedded their certification in university curricula. They conclude that 'professional HRM associations … do influence HRM curricula toward greater similarity' (2) highlighting processes of convergence internationally. The evidence suggests that the possession of recognized certification is also becoming more important to access jobs in the HRM field. Lyons et al. (2012), for instance, find that, while in 2002 only 1.4 per cent of job announcements in the USA required or preferred HR certification, by 2011 this had risen to 15.6 per cent.

less' careers and 'marketability' (Tolbert, 1996) – a topic we return to in Section 6.

4.3.3 State-Sanctioned Monopoly

Finally, trends associated with occupational licensing and registration give an indication of the outcomes of increasing professionalization efforts. As we saw, legalized professional monopolies (Freidson, 2001) have been strongly criticized by neo-liberal economists and politicians worldwide (see Section 3.2). However, evidence suggests that, in the USA, state and federal licensing has grown exponentially (Kleiner & Krueger, 2013; Kleiner & Vorotnikov, 2017). While in 1950 a mere 5 per cent of the workforce was subject to licensing requirements, by 2012 this had risen to over 32 per cent (Redbird, 2017). Indeed, in recent decades, 'occupational closure, and particularly licensure, quietly became the form for a broad swathe of U.S. occupations' (Redbird, 2017: 600). Licensing is heavily concentrated in sectors such as healthcare (over 90 per cent of the workforce), law (86 per cent), and architecture and engineering (80 per cent) but also covers many other occupations (Redbird, 2017). Given the scale of licensing, it is difficult to avoid the conclusion that it has become deeply institutionalized in the USA. Indeed, over the last forty years, only eight occupations have been successfully de-licensed (Thornton & Timmons, 2015).

Continued state support for occupational closure is evident beyond the USA. In the European Union there have been sustained efforts to limit the impact of professional monopolies. Nonetheless, occupational licensing still affects over 20 per cent of the workforce across the EU and, by some accounts, is rising (Koumenta & Pagliero, 2017). State sanctioning and support for professional claims by other means also remains strong. In the United Kindom, for example, Royal Charters date as far back as the 1750s but have increased noticeably since 2000. Only sixteen charters were issued over a twenty-year period up to 1999, compared with the thirty issued since the millennium (Kirkpatrick et al., 2017).

4.4 Conclusions

Taken together, the three trends described indicate an increasing drive by occupations to professionalize, certainly in Europe and North America. Indeed, it is hard to argue that professionalization as a route to occupational closure is in terminal decline or that the willingness of governments or employers to support professional modes of regulation has been substantially muted. Despite the force of neo-liberal critiques in recent years, the *demand* (or at least tolerance) for practitioner-led (self-)regulation continues to be strong. This is not to understate the challenges faced by the professions (see Section 3). Even when occupational closure is advanced – as with licensing – it may not guarantee economic rewards or individual autonomy for practitioners (Gorman & Sandefur, 2011). Additionally, there are signs of 'certification fatigue' on the part of employers and consumers, suggesting increasing competition between professions may lead to a 'race to the bottom' in the stringency (or lack) of enforcement of standards (Bartley, 2011). However, these caveats do not alter our overriding conclusion about the robust nature of professionalization as a viable strategy at the occupational level.

5 Professional Organizations

5.1 Introduction

In this section we turn to what might loosely be defined as a *meso* level of analysis – namely, the organizations that either directly employ or host professionals. As noted earlier, this category encompasses both autonomous and heteronomous professional organizations. However, for reasons of expediency, in this section we focus only on autonomous professional organizations and especially on private sector organizations usually labelled as Professional Services Firms (PSFs). Describing these (autonomous professional) organizations and their particular characteristics has been an important concern for organizational theorists (see Section 2). Yet, despite these contributions, questions remain, such as: how are professional services firms changing and evolving; what are the key managerial and organizational challenges they face; and what implications do these have for the structures, strategies and practices of these firms? To explore these issues, we begin by analysing broad trends with regard to the size and significance of PSFs. This leads to the related inquiry concerning the degree to which traditional modes of management and governance are evolving. Lastly, are more specific developments associated with the strategies of PSFs and processes of internationalization?

5.2 Changes in the Composition of Professional Organizations

5.2.1 PSFs: The Leading Institutional Agents of our Time

Over the past three decades, PSFs have emerged as some of the 'most rapidly growing, profitable, and significant' organizations in the global economy (Empson et al., 2015: 2) often rivalling the publicly listed corporations they service in size, geographical reach and sophistication. Indeed, the 'Big 4' accounting firms would easily be included in the *Fortune 500* list of largest companies and, by many indicators, are amongst the most globalized companies in the world, with PWC, for example, present in more countries than MacDonald's (Greenwood et al., 2006; Empson et al., 2015). Furthermore, even professions such as law and architecture – traditionally dominated by individual practitioners or small-scale family-based organizations – are now increasingly consolidated around large firms. Thus, in England and Wales, large law firms employed 40 per cent of all solicitors and generated over half of the entire profession's revenues despite representing only 2 per cent of the overall population. Ultimately, the PSF sector as a whole is of increasing economic significance, especially in advanced service-based economies such as the United Kingdom, where they account for 15 per cent of UK GDP, 14 per cent of employment and 14 per cent of exports (Financial & Legal Skills Partnership, 2018).

In the USA, the professional and business services (PBS, which excludes financial and medical services) sector also accounts for a significantly larger share of GDP (9 per cent) and employment (49 per cent) than the whole manufacturing sector (Mawdsley & Somaya, 2015).

However, it is not only a question of size and economic significance. PSFs also play a strategic role in the organization of social and economic activities

(Muzio et al., 2013; Empson et al., 2015), supporting the production, accumulation and realization of capital, lubricating the mechanisms of global capitalism and facilitating all sorts of business transactions. They act as gatekeepers in a quasi-regulatory role, as they are part of the system of checks and balances which should maintain the integrity of key societal institutions (Coffee, 2006). The Big 4 accounting firms, for instance, audit the financial information of the largest corporations in the world and guarantee their financial solidity to investors and commercial partners. Banks, actuaries and investment management firms guarantee the viability of the pension and savings system. Consultancies of various types assist firms (and public organizations) with matters ranging from improving their productivity to meeting environmental and inclusiveness standards. In short, PSFs have a pervasive influence in the operation of global capitalism (Muzio et al., 2013), to the extent that, without them, 'business as we know it would come to a grinding halt' (Sharma 1997: 758).

As highlighted in Section 3, the power and influence of (elite) PSFs also has a darker side. PSFs have facilitated some of the world's largest corporate frauds (Sikka & Willmott, 2011; Muzio et al., 2016) and have actively sought to disrupt local regulations (Arnold, 2005; Suddaby et al., 2007) and influence government's policy, arguably to their own advantage. An example of the latter are McKinsey's attempts to promote a privatization agenda in the UK healthcare system and its opposition to Obamacare in the USA (O'Mahoney & Sturdy, 2016).

All of these considerations make PSFs an increasingly important object of inquiry. Furthermore, these organizations present some unique challenges in terms of their management and organization, a theme that we explore in the remainder of this section.

5.3 Governance and Management

5.3.1 From P2 to Managed Professional Bureaucracy

Growth, internationalization and the effects of increasingly sophisticated strategies have placed a lot of pressure on the traditional practices and structures of PSFs. This is especially true with regard to their governance. The term 'governance' can be defined as 'the legal and non-legal rules, norms, conventions, standards and managerial practices that facilitate the coordination and conflict resolution amongst the critical constituencies of a professional services firm' (Leblebici & Sherer, 2015: 190). Traditionally, PSFs conformed to the P2 archetype (Greenwood et al., 1990), which, as discussed in Section 2, emphasized the values of professionalism and partnership. The concentration of ownership and control made partners jointly liable for the obligations of the firm and its management (Fama & Jensen, 1983). This system was traditionally viewed as effective because it solved the agency problem typical of corporations where ownership and control are separated and helped to limit free-rider problems (Von Nordenflycht, 2014). Through the principle of deferred gratification and up-or-out promotion (Malos & Champion, 2000), the traditional governance regime rewarded long-term commitment and contributions to the firm.

However, to manage the increasing complexity of large-scale professional organizations, traditional arrangements are being stretched and reconstituted. PSFs are adopting a so-called Managerial Professional Business (MPB) archetype, which places more emphasis on the formalization, standardization and centralization of tasks, structures and relationships (Brock et al., 1999). In terms of governance, this includes an increasing separation between the coordination and execution of work, as the management of firms becomes the responsibility of a limited number of specialized committees and managers with increasing executive powers (Empson, 2017).

Radical changes have also affected ownership structures. In particular, changes in regulation (see Section 3.4) have led to a substantial redefinition of the partnership as a form of governance. Most countries now recognize the limited liability partnership (LLP), which retains many of the fiscal advantages of the partnership but has abandoned the principle of the joint and several liability of its partners. As such, this development weakens one of the key governance features of PSFs as distinctive organizations. Joint and several liability acted as a powerful incentive for peers to monitor each other and ensure quality while promoting a strong cohesive culture and reassuring potential clients. Ongoing reforms in countries such as England and Wales or Australia are now starting to weaken this link between ownership and control by allowing firms to raise outside investment and even float into public ownership. Whilst this has certain benefits, it also negates the traditional advantages of the professional governance regimes, as already described (Greenwood & Empson, 2003; Von Nordenflycht, 2014).

In this context, a key challenge facing professional services firms is to find ways to allow them to retain some of the material and symbolic advantages of the traditional professional governance regimes whilst also (Leblebici & Sherer, 2015) adjusting to the new challenges of scale, complexity and international reach. Interestingly, some scholars (Empson, 2007; Greenwood & Empson, 2003) note how partnership as an ethos, signalling commitment to the firm and its culture as a shared enterprise, may persist in PSFs that have rejected it as a mode of governance. Examples of this include investment banks, consultancies or advertising agencies, which, although publicly listed, maintain many of the practices, symbols and discourses of the partnership model (Mckenna, 2006; Kipping, 2011).

5.4 Strategy

Another key debate around professional organizations centres on strategy (Mawdsley & Somaya, 2015, 2018). Once again, PSFs present some distinct challenges and features here relative to other types of organization. An example of this is the so-called elevator problem. This highlights the fact that, for many PSFs, key human assets are highly qualified and mobile professionals who leave every evening but, because they are hard to retain, may not return the next morning.

The first person to deal comprehensively with the issue of strategy within PSFs is David Maister (2003), who identified three strategies focused around different client work profiles and their organizational implications. These are shown in Table 7.

The brains strategy focuses on the most valuable transaction dealing with one-off unprecedented problems for which no standard solutions exist. Such work is performed by small teams of specialized (or star) professionals, with a high degree of autonomy (Brock, 2006). The grey-hair strategy deals with complex but not unprecedented transactions such as securitizations, bond emissions or corporate recovery. The final strategy (procedure) tends to deal with more routine matters. To support this, work is highly standardized and codified into organizational procedures, templates and, increasingly, knowledge management systems.

Table 7 PSF Strategy

Strategy	Brains	Gray-hair	Procedure
Type of work	One-off complex transactions	Regular transactions but highly customized	Routine transactions
Focus	Creativity and innovations	Experience and expertise	Cost efficiency
Leverage Ratio	Low	Medium	Low
Profitability	High	Medium	Low
Motto: Hire us because we are ...	Smart	Experienced	Efficient

Source: Adapted from Maister (2003).

This idea was further developed by Hansen et al. (1999) and their distinction between codification and personalization strategies. Unlike Maister, Hansen and colleagues go deeper into the organizational and managerial implications of each strategy, looking specifically at the implications for HRM, IT and Knowledge Management. Thus to give one example, codification strategies, insofar as they focus on more routinized and less lucrative transactions, tend to deploy large teams with high proportions of junior staff. This is required by the nature of the tasks, which tends to be more routine and labour intensive. HRM policies focus on the recruitment of junior staff straight out of university and on the use of internal training and development programmes with a focus on organization specific competences. Knowledge management strategies focus on the standardization, codification and routinization of competences in proprietary methodologies and technologies and on their rigid application subjected to tight project management controls (see also Suddaby & Greenwood, 2001; Brivot, 2011).

More recently, attention has shifted towards differences in service scope. Here the literature has identified a number of distinct strategies. A boutique strategy sees firms specializing in a limited number of related areas where they can retain deep reserves of expertise (Garicano & Hubbard 2007). This strategy requires a high degree of integration and is closer to Maister's (2003) notion of brain-work. Other firms may adopt a 'one stop shop' strategy (Siggelkow, 2002) which is predicated on the cross-selling and even the bundling together of multidisciplinary service packages to holistically meet clients' needs. Some of the literature reports hybrid solutions (Greenwood et al., 2005), and, whilst opinion is divided on their respective effectiveness, there seems to be a consensus that, in periods of sustained economic growth, more focused boutique strategies may be more appealing (Mawdsley & Somaya, 2015).

Overall work around strategy has the merit to capture some of the sources of distinctiveness which differentiate PSFs from other organizations and to link these to specific organizational and managerial implications. It has the further merit of drawing our attention to the significant heterogeneity of PSFs, stressing how, even within the same sector, considerable differences exist in terms of how firms position themselves in the market and organizational forms.

5.5 Internationalization

A final substantive debate that is relevant here concerns the internationalization of PSFs. As noted earlier, PSFs are on many indicators amongst the most global organizations in the world, a legacy that dates back to the nineteenth century and the age of empire. A second wave of internationalization coincided with the end of the Second World War and the arrival of US consultancy, engineering and law firms in Europe and Asia (Kipping, 2002; Dezalay & Garth, 2012). Yet, the last thirty years or so have seen a real acceleration in the international reach and intensity of professional organizations (Faulconbridge & Muzio, 2012; Boussebaa & Morgan, 2015). This has been tied to a combination of both push factors, whereby globalizing clients bring their professional advisors with them, and pull factors, as professional firms themselves seek to develop new markets on the basis of their domestic competences.

Debates in this area have focused on the strategic and organizational implications of internationalization of PSFs. In terms of organizational design, Boussebaa and Morgan (2015) identify four solutions to the challenges posed by internationalization: the project form; the network form; the federal form; and the transnational form. Project forms (Malhotra & Hinings, 2010) are usually structured around a one-off transaction such as a civil engineering project, which does not require a long-term commitment to a particular jurisdiction (a modern example would be architecture). By contrast, the network form is used by mid-size practices as a way to achieve some international reach without compromising autonomy and incurring disproportionate costs (Morgan & Quack, 2006). The federal form is a more coordinated and integrated network, where national partnerships are coordinated through a common brand and international 'umbrella' organizations. This is typical of Big 4 accounting firms (Rose & Hinings, 1999) and some large management consultancies. Finally, the transnational form is the most integrated. It has a powerful headquarters which actively coordinates all strategic and operational issues, while clients are served by global account managers to ensure consistent service (see Muzio & Faulconbridge, 2013).

The above framework raises questions about how firms balance the (often) conflicting requirements of global integration (standardizing practices, methods, cultures and structures throughout global operations) and local responsiveness. Focusing on the internationalization of English law firms in Italy, Muzio and Faulconbridge (2013; see also Faulconbridge & Muzio, 2019) identify two PSF strategies: a 'Top 3' and a 'One firm' strategy (see Table 8). The first strategy emphasizes local adaptation as much as possible and features the recruitment of local professionals, the servicing of local clients and the granting of autonomy to local offices. By contrast, the 'one firm' strategy is much more focused on global integration and on the seamless delivery of integrated and consistent services throughout the world.

Interestingly, whilst strategies vary across firms there are certain occupational and national effects at play. Thus accountants tend to adopt looser structures, as federations of national partnerships, than is the case for law

Table 8 PSFs' Internationalization Strategies

Strategy	Top 3	One Firm
Aim	Market leadership in local market	Seamless integration in global network
Global Integration	Lower	Higher
Local Responsiveness	Higher	Lower
Organizational Form	Federal	Transnational
Market Focus	Full-service	Focus on core markets
Administrative units	National subsidiaries	Transnational practice groups
Client Focus	Local and global	Multinational clients
Recruitment Policy	Locally qualified, local networks	Cosmopolitan, organizational capabilities

Source: Adapted from Muzio and Faulconbridge (2013).

firms (Rose & Hinings, 1999), whilst PSFs originating from the USA are more likely to emphasize local responsiveness than English ones (Muzio & Faulconbridge, 2013). It should also be noted that, despite the persistence of different strategies, the general trend may be one towards more integration and transnationalization (Boussebaa & Morgan, 2015), although this is often contested (Barrett et al., 2005; Boussebaa, 2009; Micelotta & Washington, 2013; Muzio & Faulconbridge, 2013) and, therefore, not always realized in practice (Faulconbridge & Muzio, 2016). Boussebaa (2009) for example, shows how differentials in salary and fee structures can hinder the creation of a globally integrated project. Similarly, Muzio and Faulconbridge (2013) show how a number of institutional differences disrupted the operations of English law firms in Italy and how this, in turn, led to the adoption of radically different business models (Faulconbridge & Muzio, 2016).

5.6 Conclusion

This section focused on the changing landscape of professional organizations, noting the increasing role and importance of PSFs as drivers and mediators of the global economy. In many ways, the professional services firm is the quintessential exemplar of the contemporary knowledge-based economy. We also saw how these organizations are undergoing (sometimes) radical change in traditional structures, practices, strategies and governance regimes. These developments highlight the need to further extend research on PSFs to understand emerging organisational forms, including those facilitated by new technology, and assess their wider impact (Malhotra et al., 2016; Smets et al., 2017).

6 Professional Workers

6.1 Introduction

Having examined professions at the occupational (labour market) and organizational level, in this section our attention shifts to the micro dimension of professional work. As well as earning higher-than-average incomes, professional workers are afforded greater freedom to determine the 'content, performance, timing, and location of their work' (Mazmanian et al., 2013: 1339). However, these assumptions are now being challenged by increased bureaucratic controls and external scrutiny. In what follows, we give an account of the size and scope of the professional workforce in Anglo-Saxon nations before turning to three core debates relating to ongoing challenges to professional autonomy, identities and career pathways.

6.2 Size, Composition and Earnings

Professional occupations constitute a prominent segment of the labour market, comprising the single largest occupational group in 2016 in the USA, the United Kingdom and Australia. This dominance is partly accounted for by the continued growth of established professions, such as in medicine and law (see Table 9 and Figure 1). It is also linked to the development of newer professions associated with the expansion of welfare states, knowledge-intensive industries and the cultural and creative sector (Švarc, 2016). The expansion of professional jobs is commensurate with an increase in earnings, particularly amongst the elite professions. For example, while mean earnings for all occupations grew by 24 per cent between 2000 and 2016 in the USA, those of physicians and surgeons increased by more than 50 per cent (see Figure 2.).

6.3 The Lived Experience of Professional Work

In this section we explore the working lives of professionals and focus our attention on three salient issues: (a) levels of practitioner autonomy; (b) the formation of professional identities; and (c) changes in career pathways.

6.3.1 Challenges to Professional Autonomy

A theme that has pervaded much of the literature on professions (see Sections 2 and 3), is the argument that professional autonomy at work is being steadily

Table 9 Doctors per 100,000 Inhabitants

	1999	2010	2015
Greece	4.3	6.2	6.3
Austria	3.8	4.8	5.1
Portugal	3.0	3.9	4.6
Norway	3.3	4.1	4.4
Germany	3.2	3.7	4.1
Spain	3.1	3.8	3.9
Denmark	2.9	3.6	3.7
Australia	2.5	*data missing*	3.5
France	3.2	3.3	3.3
Belgium	2.8	2.9	3.0
UK	1.9	2.7	2.8
USA	2.2	2.4	2.6
OECD AVERAGE	**2.8**	**0.0**	**3.4**

Source: OCED Health Statistics (2017)

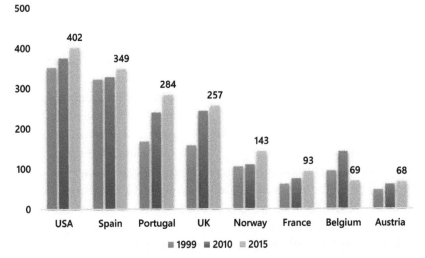

Figure 2 Lawyers per 100,000 Inhabitants. Calculated from: (a) American Bar Assoc. (2017); (b) Council of Bars and Law Societies of Europe (2015; 2010; 2008; 1999); (c) Population Reference Bureau (2016; 2010; 2001).

eroded. Typically, this threat is assumed to originate primarily from managerialism and its associated forms of control and accountability. In healthcare, for example, performance management, aimed at regulating the quality and safety of patient care, has become ever more pervasive (Kuhlmann et al., 2013).

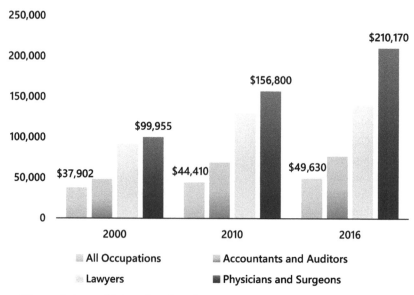

Figure 3 Annual Mean Earnings by Occupation, USA. Bureau of Labor
Statistics (2000, 2010, 2016).

Examples include evidence-based medicine and new clinical guidelines (Adler
and Kwon, 2013) which seek to prescribe practice and limit the discretion that
individual clinicians exercise on a case-by-case basis (Martin et al., 2017).

Professionals working in PSFs have also been subjected to greater managerial
and bureaucratic control. For example, new technologies have been deployed to
monitor practitioners to ensure that client assignments are delivered 'within, or
under, budget' (Anderson-Gough et al., 2000: 1160). In many PSFs there is also a
greater reliance on precedents, diagnostic methodologies, toolkits, templates and
standardized 'boilerplate' solutions (Gulati & Scott, 2012). These tendencies have
advanced even further in less professionalized fields such as management consulting. Kipping and Kirkpatrick (2013), for example, observe how the practices of
earlier (and smaller) engineering and strategy consulting firms were dislodged by
high leverage ratios and codified knowledge management systems upon which the
recent wave of IT and outsourcing consultancies developed their business model. A
related change is the creation of dedicated managerial roles filled by both specialist
and hybrid professional-managers. For some, this amounts to the 'corporatization'
of professional practice (Empson & Langley 2015), although opinions differ on the
impact of these new forms of managerial authority.

New accountability regimes represent a further assumed threat to practitioner
autonomy. An example of this would be computerized time-management and
billing systems (Campbell & Charlesworth, 2012). By recording the activities

of practitioners on six-minute intervals, these systems instil self-discipline amongst practitioners to maximize productivity and, it is hoped, firm profitability (Thornton, 2016).

The preceding discussion suggests that professional work is subject to greater levels of control than in the past. Performance targets, financial controls and standardized work processes are some of the developments curtailing practitioners' ability to exercise discretion, over both the means (and especially) ends of their work. Nonetheless, the impact of these developments should not be overstated. Empirical studies point to the tactics employed by practitioners to reassert their operational autonomy or emphasize the limitations of standardized work processes (Campbell & Charlesworth, 2012; Faulconbridge & Muzio, 2008).

6.3.2 Inequality and Exclusion

Employment growth in elite professions has been sustained by an increase in female and in Black, Asian, and Minority Ethnic (BAME) practitioners. Globally, the entry of women in many professions is similar to, or exceeds, the entry rate for men (Sommerlad & Ashley, 2015). The growth in numbers, however, has not resulted in equal career outcomes. Whilst the make-up of most professions is more diverse than twenty years ago, women and minorities still often find themselves clustered in lower-grade roles and specialisms (Bolton & Muzio, 2008). For example, in 2015, 49 per cent of solicitors in England and Wales were women, but only 22 per cent of partners (The Law Society, 2016). The proportion of female partners is even lower in the most prestigious firms, with the percentage in top-tier elite firms dwindling to less than 10 per cent (Sommerlad & Ashley, 2015). Similar patterns are evident in other elite professions such as medicine and accountancy (AICPA, 2017).

Scholarship directed at uncovering the explanations for unequal career outcomes is vast (Gorman, 2015) and includes studies examining how workplace structures, values and practices convey neutrality whilst favouring some groups over others. Drawing on the notion of occupational closure (discussed in Section 2) Wilkins and Gulati (1996) suggest that traditional career structures are gendered and racially biased. This means that professionals from minority groups are less likely to receive the type of work, training and supervision necessary to succeed. Similarly, while billable hours constitute a core criterion for advancement in many PSFs, the means by which client assignments are allocated and performance measured disadvantages women (Bolton & Muzio, 2008).

The existence of implicit biases which exaggerate in-group favouritism (Gorman, 2005) is a further reason why career outcomes for women and

BAME practitioners tend to lag behind those of white men. Kmec and Gorman note an 'increasing disadvantage for women as they climb organizational hierarchies' (2009: 1465) due to the cognitive biases of senior decision-makers. For instance, affinity bias – the tendency to develop relationships with people from a similar background – encourages actors in leadership positions to invest more resources in practitioners with a similar background. Similarly, 'typecasting' tends to cluster women and minorities in areas of work congruent with their assumed abilities (Rhode, 2015). Therefore, partly for these reasons, professional organizations can operate as 'inequality regimes' (Acker, 2006) whereby class ceilings (Friedman et al., 2015), mommy tracks (Noonan & Corcoran, 2004) and occupational ghettos (Charles & Grusky, 2004) disproportionately affect the working conditions and lived experiences of some groups. While many PSFs have initiatives addressing inequality (Ashley & Empson, 2013), progress is slow and fraught with difficulties (Sommerlad & Ashley, 2015). Indeed, Kornberger et al.'s (2010: 788) study of the effects of a flexibility program at Sky Accounting found that, despite 'the genuine intentions of its sponsors', the programme 'actually deepened' gender barriers, resulting in a marginal decline in the percentage of female directors over a seven-year period from its inception.

6.3.3 Overwork and Well-Being

Overworking has become a common feature of professional work (Lupu & Empson, 2015). Specifically, overworking encompasses three aspects: intensification (working harder); extensification (working longer); and its encroachment into the personal sphere, blurring previously clear boundaries between work and home (Mazmanian et al., 2013). A growing body of international research reveals that sustained periods of overworking are adversely affecting professionals' physical and mental health. For example, in the largest study of its kind since the 1990s, research co-funded by the American Bar Association reveals high levels of alcohol abuse, depression and anxiety among US attorneys (Krill et al., 2016).

Overwork might result from organizational controls that are sometimes subtle or indirect – such as the billable hours system (Campbell & Charlesworth, 2012). It may also be attributable to personal choice or at least the illusion of choice (Lupu & Empson, 2015). Technology is a further factor that contributes to overwork. Constant internet connectivity makes it harder for practitioners to resist expectations of 24/7 availability. As Mazmanian et al. (2013) found, professional workers equated autonomy with the freedom to choose *where* to work rather than *if* they work. Thus, even though the use of mobile e-mail devices resulted in work spilling over into evenings and weekends, professional workers viewed this as personal choice. In a separate study focusing on why partners and leaders work excessively, Lupu and Empson (2015) conclude that it is precisely because these practitioners are successful (and fear loss of status) that they feel compelled to overwork.

6.4 Professional Identities

Professional identity comprises the 'constellation of attributes, beliefs, values, motives, and experiences' by which individuals define themselves in their professional role and how they act in work situations (Ibarra, 1999: 764–5). Early sociological studies, such as *Boys in White* (an account of the socialization of medical residents) (Becker et al., 1961), tended to view professional identity as 'relatively stable, structured, enduring, and resilient' (Lepisto et al., 2015: 12). Education and on-the-job training are critical processes by which would-be practitioners develop their professional identity and are socialized to become members of their chosen occupation (Bechky, 2011; Van Maanen & Barley, 1984).

Yet, while the influence of occupational communities is powerful, recent scholarship views professional identity as inherently malleable, fluid and subject to continual 'work' (Gill, 2015). Professional workers are seen as agents engaged in ongoing mental activity to create, maintain, modify and, generally, craft a sense of self. Ibarra's (1999) study of junior consultants and investment bankers transitioning to a new advisory role is one of the earliest exploring this fluidity. By observing role models, junior professionals developed a repertoire of tacit knowledge, behaviour, routines and demeanour to create a 'provisional self' congruent with an image of their desired self. Professional workers refined their makeshift identities by adding, discarding and revising elements of their repertoire until the provisional self became an authentic identity.

Recently, attention has focused on organizational and institutional influences on the formation of professional identities. Drawing on Foucauldian notions of disciplinary power (see also Section 2), scholarship has sought to show how managerial control in PSFs is exercised through 'identity regulation' (Alvesson & Willmott, 2002: 625). Here, professional identity is defined less in terms of occupational norms but is purposefully managed to encourage behaviour aligned with corporate priorities (Kornberger et al., 2011). These processes may be substituting the occupational community with the firm as the primary source of professional socialization and identity construction. An example is Grey's (1994) account of how the very notion of a 'professional career' is shaped largely by in-house training programmes, appraisals and other HRM practices. The role of 'disciplining techniques' in forming partner identity is also highlighted by Covaleski et al.'s (1998) study of 'Big 6' accounting firms. They found that management by objectives and mentoring acted as surveillance tools that shaped individual subjectivities and helped transform autonomous professionals into 'corporate clones'.

Processes of identity regulation can also be driven by wider changes in the institutional environment of the professions. A number of studies have explored this dimension, looking at how professions negotiate and adapt to field level pressures. Goodrick and Reay (2010), for example, focus on how new forms of professional identity are discursively legitimated, in the case of registered nurses. Chreim et al. (2007) also look at how the institutional environment may provide resources that both constrain and enable professionals as they reshape their professional identities. Most recently, Kyratsis et al. (2017) focus on the different tactics by which doctors sought to change their identities following the ascendency of a new professional logic in primary care medicine in five (transitioning) European healthcare systems. Their study illustrates how the 'identity work' of doctors – authenticating, reframing and cultural re-positioning – is critical for understanding how new healthcare practices or logics are translated and 'enacted at a local level' (636).

6.5 Professional Careers

For individual practitioners, careers are the conduit through which 'the benefits of professional life (status and income) are accrued' (Leicht & Fennell, 1997: 22) and the means through which personal expertise and reputation is continuously developed. Because professional workers are central to the creation of value, the career model by which this labour is attracted, motivated and retained is also of paramount importance to organizations such as PSFs (Smets et al., 2011). Traditionally, recruitment and progression practices in PSFs assumed the form of an 'up-or-out' promotion tournament (Galanter & Palay, 1991). Recruiting only from elite universities, associates were placed on a 'partnership track' where they received expert mentoring and training for a fixed term after which they competed with fellow associates for a small number of partnership positions. Assessments were based on candidates' relative ranking within the cohort rather than absolute performance. Those who were successful became co-owners of the firm, the benefits of which included job security, professional status and 'a lifetime of steadily increasing earnings unmatched … in the other learned professions' (cf. Galanter & Palay 1991: 42). Unsuccessful candidates exited the firm voluntarily or were dismissed. In its purest form, the model established an internal labour market comprising two positions: associates and partners (Maister, 2003).

Designed to be a self-sustaining meritocracy by Paul Cravath in the early 1900s, the up-or-out tournament became widely diffused across all professional service types, geographies and firm sizes (Morris & Pinnington, 1998). While the tournament is assumed to benefit PSFs, inevitably it contributes to high levels of staff turnover (Iyer et al., 2000). Various strategies are deployed to manage this, including enacting personnel policies that foster strong organizational affiliation amongst practitioners during their term of employment and instituting alumni relations programmes that ensure organizational identification is sustained upon leaving (Iyer et al., 2000).

However, the promotion to partnership tournament is now changing (Malhotra et al., 2010). The model assumes that associates compete in the tournament because they regard the deferred reward – partnership – as valuable and achievable. Yet there are indications that many younger professionals are increasingly sceptical of 'partnership' as the ultimate career objective. Keen to pursue interests outside work, so-called millenials are satisfied with roles that at one time would have been viewed as a sign of failure (Malhotra et al., 2016: 374). The legitimacy of the up-or-out model has also been challenged by diversity, inclusion and equality discourses which highlight the disadvantages of the tournament model for certain groups (Kay et al., 2013; Ashley & Empson, 2013). These developments are liable to accentuate turnover rates in PSFs (Bidwell & Briscoe, 2010) and could further undermine the tournament model in future (Malhotra et al., 2016: 369).

In response to these challenges, many PSFs have sought to reform career practices in three ways. First, two-tier partnership structures have been introduced as a way of rewarding employees without diluting profits (Ackroyd & Muzio, 2007). Second, firms have established tenured, mid-career non-partnership positions that promise greater work–life balance so as to minimize turnover (Malhotra et al., 2010; 2016). Examples include 'Professional Support Lawyer' in law and 'Permanent Senior Associate' in accounting firms (Smets et al., 2017). Finally, by outsourcing and/or offshoring professional services (Sako, 2015), firms have substantively reduced graduate recruitment (Kuruvilla & Noronha 2015). These innovations have, inadvertently 'reinforced the traditional partnership ... as the norm' (Smets et al., 2017: 100).

Alongside new career pathways in traditional PSFs, new career types are also evident in alternative settings such as 'network-based' PSFs (Gardner & Eccles, 2011). Here, professionals work as freelancers, assigned to work tasks in accordance to their skills and, importantly, their personal choice (Christensen et al., 2013). In this context, new technologies may support practitioners interested in pursuing a freelancing career. The Gerson Lehrman Group, for example, connects its online network of 400,000 experts to clients seeking on-demand advice (Susskind & Susskind, 2015).

Theoretically, these patterns of working highlight the development of so-called boundaryless or protean careers. Not tied to a single organization, individuals self-direct their careers in line with personal values and choices. Theorists view 'boundaryless' careers as a response to two developments: (i) the disintegration of internal labour markets; and (ii) an intensification of work. Thus, it is argued that, because organizations no longer guarantee employment as they once did (Tolbert, 1996), professionals attain greater security by working as contractors or freelancers, moving freely between organizations on a project-by-project basis (Barley & Kunda, 2004).

Boundaryless careers may also be understood as a response to organisational and work pressures. Focusing on social work, for example, Kirkpatrick & Hoque (2006) note how temporary agency working was motivated by a desire to 'escape' from permanent employment. The idea of escaping the shackles of employment and regaining control of one's own career has also featured strongly in recruitment campaigns by alternative professional service providers. Keystone Law's installation of what looked like an exhausted lawyer, imprisoned in a cage at one of London's busiest railway stations, attracted – as intended – much media attention (Keystone Law, 2015). These tendencies however, should not be over-exaggerated. In the United Kingdom, the proportion of practitioners working as freelancers in the professional services occupational grouping in 2016 was still only 11 per cent (Jenkins, 2017).

6.6 Conclusion

This chapter shows that professional occupations constitute a prominent segment of the labour market. On average, they earn the highest salaries, account for the largest share of employment across all groups, and, despite the predictions that new technologies will displace professional labour (see Section 3.3), it is these occupations that will generate most of the jobs in future. Nonetheless, organizational responses to macro-developments have a direct bearing on practitioners' lived experience of work, with work intensification a primary example. Yet, it is essential to avoid casting professional workers as over-socialized 'dupes' with little agency. By making sense of, negotiating and responding to the organizational context in which they are located, other scholarship has drawn attention to ways in which professional workers are highly adept at developing strategies to respond to emergent challenges and exploiting the opportunities presented by them (Evetts, 2011).

7 Conclusions

Our point of departure for this Element was the assertion that professional forms of regulation and the (professional) organizations associated with this have become increasingly important in contemporary society. Yet, we also noted how these institutions have been subject to challenges and that professionalism, as a distinct work organizational principle, may be under attack (Freidson, 2001; Leicht, 2016). Key sources of entropy include changes in social attitudes towards expertise, the development of new technologies and the shifting relationship between governments and professions, undermining and weakening traditional arrangements such as monopoly and self-regulation. As such, practices, routines and activities once reflective of professionalism have been threatened by newer market and organizational logics (Thornton & Ocasio, 1999; Thornton, 2002). The global financial crisis (Harvey, 2010) has also represented a pivotal turning point in how professional work is performed, with a direct bearing on practitioners' lived experiences. One effect of this is that expert work has become hyper-intensified, facilitated by the deployment of new technologies. Far from self-actualizing, professionals, in many ways, have become over-worked cyborgs, emotionally exhausted, alienated, insecure and dissatisfied (Muhr, 2011).

However, while these challenges are very real, in this Element we have tried to provide a more balanced narrative, one that also acknowledges the resilient and adaptable nature of the professions. A central argument we have tried to convey is about the underlying resilience and vitality of the professions, their modes of governance and strategies in contemporary society. While these institutions are certainly evolving and changing, they are not, we argue, in a state of decay or decline.

To develop these arguments, we have adopted an approach which is distinctive compared to other recent treatments of this topic. First, we have highlighted the importance of focusing *both* on the role of professions as occupations and actors in the wider societal arena (professionalization) and professional organizations. The former draws attention to professionalism as a distinctive way of organizing in the labour market, whereby members of an occupation rather than consumers or employers retain control over the definition, performance and evaluation of their work. By contrast, the latter is concerned with the organizations of professions (such as membership associations) and formal organizations that employ or host professionals (such as PSFs). This means focusing on the agency of professions in the formation of organizational practices and on the wider development of organizational fields. However, also implied is the role of organizations as actors in the formation of professions (Brint, 1994), a theme which has often been neglected in the literature. Burrage and Torstendahl (1990), for example, famously identified four key 'actors' in the development of professions – practicing members, users, the state and universities – but say little when it comes to the distinctive role of employing organizations. In this Element we have sought to provide a different account, one which highlights not only the role that organizations may have on the work and occupational identity of individual professionals (Section 6) but also how organizations (such as PSFs) might (directly or indirectly) influence the emerging strategies of professions.

A second distinctive feature of our approach is the framing of theoretical debates about the professions using *three* lenses: functional, power and institution. These lenses provide a roadmap for navigating the extensive literature on the sociology of professions and how it has developed over the previous sixty years. However, while there are some overlaps with earlier overviews of the topic (MacDonald, 1995; Anteby et al., 2016), by highlighting the contributions of institutional theory this Element also develops a taxonomy that is significantly different (Muzio et al., 2013). The addition of an institution lens, we argue, is important for advancing and revitalizing the sociology of professions, highlighting new insights and directions for research. As we saw, the institutional lens looks beyond the specific concerns of professions as occupations focused on the narrow objective of achieving closure and labour market exclusivity. From this perspective, professions are also 'cultural producers' helping to reinforce a common sense of identity within occupational communities and to disseminate knowledge and practice. This insight also draws attention to the wider role of professions as 'entrepreneurs' responsible for the wider development of societal institutions (Scott, 2008). As Suddaby and Viale (2011: 423) suggest, 'professional projects carry with them projects of institutionalization'. Hence, the institutional perspective offers a way of significantly broadening the focus of the sociology of professions, emphasizing the dynamic agency of professions both in the pursuit of their own collective interests *and* in the construction of organizational fields and societal institutions more generally.

A third way in which this Element departs from previous work is in how it frames contemporary debates about what is happening to the professions. Building on other recent accounts, we have sought to articulate three primary challenges that are potentially undermining the hegemony of professions and professional organizations: cultural de-legitimization, the disruptive potential of new technologies and new modes of regulation (or re-regulation). These challenges are articulated in some detail in Section 3. However, our analysis also provides a way of understanding how these challenges manifest themselves at different levels: macro, meso and micro. This means exploring change at the level of occupations (Section 4), within professional organizations (such as PSFs) (Section 5) and individual professionals in the workplace (Section 6). As can be seen in Table 10, it is possible to

Table 10 Multidimensional Nature of Challenges

	Cultural demystification	New technology	Re-regulation
Macro – Occupations	Declining public trust Cynicism in the ethical standards of professional associations and their willingness to deal with misconduct	Precipitates the disappearance of some occupations and emergence of others	State control, declining powers to self-regulate in terms of production of producers Challenges to principle of professional monopoly
Meso – Organizations	Client led demands for accountability and transparency of providers (litigation) Impact on firm status and reputation	Rise of new competitors Re-organization of services Changing skill mix Facilitating new knowledge and services transfer	New governance regulation and growing emphasis on firms as agents accountable for enacting, internalizing regulatory demands
Micro – Individuals	Changing relationships, with (more assertive) clients, weakening status and identity of the professional expert	Declining autonomy and discretion Work intensification	Increased accountability and transparency Reporting demands Performance management

combine these two dimensions to articulate the *multidimensional* nature of the challenges facing contemporary professions.

7.1 Contemporary Significance of Professions and Future Research

Adopting this approach, we have sought to critically review the theory and research on professions to provide a roadmap for scholars and practitioners. However, as noted earlier, our goal has also been to further contribute to debates on this topic and frame them in a different way. Specifically, our goal has been to articulate *three core messages* about the contemporary significance of professions, about how they are evolving and about how they should be studied.

7.1.1 Centrality of Professions and Professionalization as Institutions

The first core message is simply to draw attention to the continued centrality and vitality of professions and professionalization as institutions. In this regard, our message contrasts with many grand narratives of professions as embattled, increasingly irrelevant legacies from a pre-industrial era of craft guilds and gentlemen's clubs (Krause, 1996; Broadbent et al., 1997; Reed, 1996; 2007). Such an image, we argue, is both misplaced and potentially counterproductive. Above all, it significantly understates the continued importance of professions and the stability of professional forms of regulation. This is indicated by employment trends, for example, with professions in the USA now representing the fastest-growing occupational group (representing 21 per cent of the work-force) (see Section 6). The image of terminal decline is also out of sync with the trends noted in Section 4 regarding the exponential growth of professional certification and, in the USA, state licensing – which now covers over 32 per cent of the workforce (Redbird, 2017). These trends highlight the continued (indeed growing) significance of occupational closure as a form of labour market regulation and its widening appeal to occupations beyond the more established fields of law, education and healthcare. While, as we saw in Section 3, governments around the world have been influenced by neo-liberal arguments about the risks of professional monopoly, so far this has not translated into any meaningful reduction in support for older regulatory practices.

Trends relating to organizations also highlight the continued significance of professions. The population of professional membership associations has expanded in the USA and elsewhere, suggesting that occupations are becoming 'more organized', while the size, geographical reach and sophistication of PSFs was detailed in Section 5. By recording these trends, we have tried to emphasize the ubiquity of professions. Their influence relates not just to the regulation of expert work and control over expert service provision but to its status as one of the preeminent institutional agents of our time (Scott, 2008: 219). This draws attention to the power that professionals (and their organizations) wield as key problem-solvers in an increasingly complex knowledge economy. It also relates to the dark side of professions and the need for continued vigilance in the face of risks associated with incompetence and unethical behaviour.

7.1.2 Continual Evolution of Professional Organizations and Modes of Regulation

Our second key message stems directly from the first and is concerned with how professional organizations and modes of regulation are evolving. Important here are the adaptive capabilities of professions (Abbott, 1988). It is essential to avoid viewing professional workers as over-socialized 'puppets' or 'dupes' (Greenwood et al., 2015) with little agency. Rather, by making sense of, negotiating with and responding to the organizational context in which they are located, scholarship draws attention to ways in which professional workers and organizations are highly adept at forging strategies to respond to emergent challenges and exploiting the opportunities presented by them (Ackroyd, 1996; Evetts, 2014; Currie et al., 2012).

This emphasis on the adaptive capabilities of professions has led some to refer to broader processes of re-configuration or hybridization (Noordegraaf, 2011; Adler et al., 2008). Hence, Adler et al. (2008) notes how (long) established models of 'professional community' are being reformed in ways that adjust to the needs of hierarchies and markets. This is leading to an alternative form of 'collaborative community', which is better equipped for responding to contemporary demands. Noordegraaf (2011) has also drawn attention to how professions are being 'reconfigured' in response to new pressures in their environment: the emergence of what he terms 'wicked cases', changing risk perceptions and demographic shifts.

In this Element, we have sought to highlight similar evolutionary tendencies. These are apparent across all three levels of analysis, the macro, meso and micro. Hence, as we saw in Section 4, while forms of occupational closure appear robust, with continued support for state licensing, there are signs that achieving closure, in itself, may be increasingly insufficient to guarantee financial rewards, status or increased autonomy. If anything, the latter may be reduced in a context of declining public trust in professions, respect for expertise and the erosion of professional freedoms to regulate themselves. As such, while the institutions of occupational closure remain robust in formal terms, it is possible that they are also losing their potency and are, to some extent, being hollowed out.

A very similar argument about continuity and change applies to professional organizations (explored in Section 5). These organizations (notably PSFs) have grown in size and importance. In many ways, they retain many of their distinctive hallmarks, including an emphasis on practitioner autonomy and aspects of collegial decision-making. However, it is clear that the model of 'professional organization' is evolving. This is evidenced by the trends described in Section 5, such as changes in governance, the growth of private investment, the erosion of the partnership model and the role that firms play in reshaping the socialization and identity of practitioners. In the long term, this may be leading to more 'managed' forms of professional organization, which are quite different from the loosely controlled professional bureaucracies of the past.

7.1.3 Continued Value of Concepts from the Sociology of Professions

Lastly, in this Element we have tried to emphasize the continued vitality and usefulness and ideas from the sociology of professions (SOP). In doing so, we recognize that such a claim may be unfashionable. According to Gorman and Sandefur (2011), the 'golden age' of the SOP in the 1960s is now long past. This literature, they suggest, has become increasingly 'quiescent' in recent times, characterized by 'outdated theoretical frameworks that no longer hold much appeal' (276). Needless to say, in this Element we strongly disagree with this assessment. As can be seen from much of the literature reviewed, interest in the professions as a phenomenon remains strong. This is apparent from the burgeoning research on PSFs (Empson et al., 2015; Smets et al., 2017) and from the establishment of periodicals, such as the *Journal of Professions and Organizations*, which are dedicated to advancing the field.

More importantly, as we have tried to show in Section 2, there is also great scope to advance the field by linking insights from the sociology of professions literature to institutional theory. This synthesis, we argue, points to new ways of exploring professions, not just as occupations but as agents of wider societal and institutional change. The field might also be enhanced by incorporating the sociology of professions within a more inclusive 'sociology of expertise' (Eyal 2013). The latter, according to Eyal, asks 'not only who controls a task and how jurisdictional boundaries are assembled but also what arrangements, devices, concepts, and other actors are necessary if an expert statement or performance is to be formulated, reproduced, and disseminated as an immutable and combinable mobile' (899). This approach implies focusing both on practices and wider networks of relationships which include professionals, non-professionals and users.

7.2 Future Directions

Of course, when arriving at these conclusions, it is always useful to reflect on limitations and possible directions for future research. This Element has drawn almost exclusively from available secondary sources taken from diverse strands in this literature. As such, there is obvious potential to develop these arguments through further empirical research to validate and better understand some of the trends we have identified. We suggested that research might usefully combine insights from the SOP and institutional theory and a more inclusive understanding of how 'professional' expertise is enacted through wider networks and relationships. It might also make greater use of longitudinal data, for example from archival sources or the kind of quantitative data sets deployed in Sections 4 and 6.

Specific avenues for future research are suggested by the debates profiled in Sections 4, 5 and 6, focusing on the macro, meso and micro worlds of the professions. With regard to the occupational dimension (Section 4), for example, it would be useful to understand more about why professionalization strategies appear to be so resilient. Attention might also investigate the consequences of extended professional regulation in some fields, for consumers and producers (practicing professionals themselves). Turning to professional organisations (Section 5), an interesting question concerns the role of new technology in promoting alternative forms of network organisation where stakeholders are redrawn so as to facilitate multidisciplinary solutions and the co-production of services. A further line of research might focus on the extent to which new technology, regulations and market demands are altering power relationships within and between professional firms. Lastly, building on these themes, we need to know more about how the increasing diversity of organizational forms and work settings (associated with the so-called gig economy) impacts on how professionals experience work (Pichault & McKeown, 2019). Future research in this area could also explore the implications of changing work environments for how professions understand the notion of careers and career progression and the notion of professional identity.

Beyond these specific concerns, we think that a useful way forward is to explore the relationships between professions (as occupations) and organizations more generally. While these have sometimes been viewed as relatively independent domains of research (Lounsbury, 2007), we have highlighted the need to combine them in a more dynamic way. Finally, there is considerable scope to explore the changing dynamics of professions across different settings and in a transnational context. We have explored the latter in relation to global PSFs (see Section 5). However, more attention might also be given to forms of occupational regulation that are transnational (Samsonova-Taddei & Humphrey, 2014).

Furthermore, professions are beginning to develop in fast-emerging economies, notably China and India. Whether traditional notions of the concept of professionalism are relevant in these settings warrants research, as does the role of the state and ways in which it might be fashioning professional projects, professional ideology and its practice. Indeed, an emergent strand of scholarship is directed towards addressing gaps in our knowledge that have arisen from traditional analyses focused on Anglo-American professions. Bonnin and Ruggunan (2016) examine recent developments in professions in South Africa, such as strategies by which the state and professional bodies have sought to alter the racial composition of traditional professions. The theme of transformation, access and the removal of barriers is also explored by Ballakrishnen (2016), who traces the organization and emergence of three different, but related, high-status professional spaces in India: law, management consulting and information technology. These and other studies highlight the need to further widen the scope of research to understand global trends and enrich our understanding of professions and their strategies as they evolve in different national and cultural contexts.

References

Abbott, A. (1988) *The System of Professions: An Essay on the Division of Expert Labor.* Chicago, IL: University of Chicago Press.

Abel, R. L. (1988) *The Legal Profession in England and Wales.* New York: Blackwell.

Acker, A. (2006) Inequality Regimes: Gender, Class, and Race in Organizations. *Gender and Society* 2(4): 441–64.

Ackroyd, S. (1996) Organization contra organizations: professions and organizational change in the United Kingdom. *Organization Studies* 17(4): 599–621.

Ackroyd, S. (2016) Sociological and organizational theories of professions and professionalism. In M. Dent, I. Bourgeault, J-L. Denis and E. Kuhlmann (eds.), *The Routledge Companion to the Professions and Professionalism.* London: Taylor and Francis, pp. 15–30.

Ackroyd, S., and Muzio, D. (2007) The reconstructed professional firm: explaining change in English legal practices. *Organization Studies* 28(5): 729–47.

Ackroyd, S., Kirkpatrick, I., and Walker, R. M. (2007) Public management reform in the UK and its consequences for professional organization: a comparative analysis. *Public Administration* 85(1): 9–26.

Adams, T. L. (2017) Self-regulating professions: past, present, future. *Journal of Professions and Organization* 4(1): 70–87.

Adler, P. S., and Kwon, S. W. (2013) The mutation of professionalism as a contested diffusion process: clinical guidelines as carriers of institutional change in medicine. *Journal of Management Studies* 50(5): 930–62.

Adler, P., Kwon, S., and Hecksher, C. (2008) Professional work: the emergence of collaborative community. *Organization Science* 19(2): 359–76.

AICPA (2017) *Trends in the Supply of Accounting Graduates and the Demand for Public Accounting Recruits.* Durham, NC: Association of International Certified Professional Accountants. http://bit.ly/2PF9grQ.

Albert, K. W. (2017) Research Note: Trends in the Demographics of College-Educated Professional Association Members in the United States, 1993–2015. Unpublished, on file with authors.

Albert, K. W. (2015) Professional associations and certification: A divergence of professional and cccupational interests. Paper presented to Society for the Advancement of Socio-Economics, London, 2–4 July. http://bit.ly/2ALsK6o.

Alvesson, M., and Willmott, H. (2002) Identity regulation as organizational control: producing the appropriate individual. *Journal of Management Studies* 39(5): 619–44.

American Bar Association (2017) *American Bar Association National Lawyer Population Survey: Historical Trends in Total National Lawyer Population 1878–2017.* http://bit.ly/2qqRPAh

Anderson-Gough, F., Grey, C., and Robson, K. (2000) In the name of the client: the service ethic in two professional services firms. *Human Relations* 53(9): 1151–74.

Anderson-Gough, F., Grey, C., and Robson, K. (2005). Helping them to forget: the organizational embedding of gender relations in public audit firms. *Accounting, Organizations and Society* 30(5): 469–90.

Anteby, M. (2010) Markets, morals, and practices of trade: jurisdictional disputes in the U.S. commerce in cadavers. *Administrative Science Quarterly* 55: 606–38.

Anteby, M., Chan, C. K., and DiBenigno, J. (2016) Three lenses on occupations and professions in organizations: becoming, doing, and relating. *Academy of Management Annals* 10(1): 183–244.

Armstrong, P. (2000) Changing management control strategies – the role of competition between accountancy and other organizational professions. In J. R. Edwards (ed.), *History of Accounting: Critical Perspectives in Business and Management* (Vol. IV). London: Routledge.

Arnold, J. (2005) *Work Psychology: Understanding Human Behaviour in the Workplace*, 4th ed. London: Prentice Hall Financial Time.

Arronowitz, S., and DiFazio, W. (1995) *The Jobless Future*, 2nd ed. Minneapolis: University of Minnesota Press.

Ashley, L., and Empson, L. (2013) Differentiation and discrimination: understanding social class and social exclusion in leading law firms. *Human Relations* 66(2): 219–44.

Australian Trade Practices Commission (TPC) (1993) *National Competition Policy Report, Hilmer Report.* http://bit.ly/2nnSd4b.

Ballakrishnen, S. (2016) India (International) Inc.: global work and the (re-) organization of professionalism in emerging economies. In M. Dent, I. Bourgeault, J-L. Denis and E. Kuhlmann (eds.), *The Routledge Companion to the Professions and Professionalism.* London: Routledge, pp. 265–79.

Barley, S., and Tolbert, P. S. (1991) An introduction: at the intersection of organizations and occupations. In P. S. Tolbert and S. Barley (eds.), *Research in the Sociology of Organizations* (Vol. 8). Cheltenham: Emerald Publishing, 1–13.

Barley, S. R., and Kunda, G. (2004) *Gurus, Hired Guns, and Warm Bodies: Itinerant Experts in a Knowledge Economy.* Princeton, NJ: Princeton University Press.

Barney, J. B. (1991) Firm resources and sustained competitive advantage. *Journal of Management* 17(1): 99–120.

Barrett, M., Cooper, D. J., and Jamal, K. (2005) Globalization and the coordinating of work in multinational audits. *Accounting, Organizations and Society* 30(1): 1–24.

Bartley, T. (2011) Certification as a mode of social regulation. In D. Levi-Faur (ed.), *Handbook on the Politics of Regulation*. Cheltenham: Edward Elgar, pp. 441–52. Previously Jerusalem Papers in Regulation & Governance Working Paper No. 8.

Bechky, B. A. (2003) Sharing meaning across occupational communities: the transformation of understanding on a production floor. *Organization Science* 14(3): 312–30.

Bechky, B. A. (2011) Making organizational theory work: institutions, occupations, and negotiated orders. *Organization Science* 22(5): 1157–67.

Becker, H. (1970) *Sociological Work: Method and Substance*. Piscataway, NJ: Transaction Books.

Becker, H. F., Geer, B., Hughes, E. C., and Strauss, A. L. (1961) *Boys in White*. Chicago, IL: University of Chicago Press.

Bell, D. (1973) *The Coming of Post-Industrial Society: A Venture in Social Forecasting*. New York: Basic Books.

Bevan, G., and Hood, C. (2006) What's measured is what matters: targets and gaming in the English public health care system. *Public Administration* 84 (3): 517–38.

Bidwell, M., and Briscoe, F. (2010) The dynamics of interorganizational careers. *Organization Science* 21(5): 1034–53.

Birkett, W. P., and Evans, E. (2005) Theorizing professionalization: a model for organizing and understanding histories of the professionalizing activities of occupational associations of accountants. *Accounting History* 10(1): 99–127.

Blau, P., and Scott, W. R. (1962) *Formal Organizations: A Comparative Approach*. Stanford, CA: Stanford University Press.

Bol, T. (2014) Economic returns to occupational closure in the German skilled trades. *Social Science Research* 46: 9–22.

Bolton, S., and Muzio, D. (2008) The paradoxical processes of feminization in the professions: the case of established, aspiring and semi-professions. *Work, Employment and Society* 22(2): 281–99.

Bonnin, D., and Ruggunan, S. (2016) Professions and professionalism in emerging economies: the case of South Africa. In M. Dent, I. Bourgeault, J-L. Denis and E. Kuhlmann (eds.), *The Routledge Companion to the Professions and Professionalism*. London: Routledge, pp. 251–64.

Boussebaa, M. (2009) Struggling to organize across national borders: the case of global resource management in professional service firms. *Human Relations* 62(6): 829–50.

Boussebaa, M., and Morgan, G. (2015) The internationalization of professional service firms: drivers, forms and outcomes. In L. Empson, D. Muzio, J. Broschack and B. Hinings (eds.), *The Oxford Handbook of Professional Services Firms*. Oxford: Oxford University Press, pp. 71–91.

Braverman, H. (1974) *Labour and Monopoly Capital*. New York: Monthly Review Press.

Brint, S. G. (1994) *In an Age of Experts: The Changing Role of Professionals in Politics and Public Life*. Princeton, NJ: Princeton University Press.

British Office of Fair Trading (2001) *Competition in Professions*. http://bit.ly/2BEVuPq.

Brivot, M. (2011) Controls of knowledge production, sharing and use in bureaucratized professional service firms. *Organization Studies* 32(4): 489–508.

Broadbent, J., Dietrich, M., and Roberts, J. (1997) *The End of the Professions? The Restructuring of Professional Work*. London: Routledge.

Brock, D. M. (2006) The changing professional organization: A review of competing archetypes. *International Journal of Management Reviews* 8(3), 157–74.

Brock, D. M., Powell, M. J., and Hinings, C. R. (1999) The restructured professional organization: corporates, cobwebs and cowboys. In M. J. Powell, D. M. Brock and C. R. Hinings (eds), *Restructuring the Professional Organization: Accounting Health Care and Law*. London: Routledge, pp. 215–29.

Broschak, J. (2015) Client relationships in professional service firms. In L. Empson et al. (eds.), *Oxford Handbook of Professional Service Firms*. Oxford: Oxford University Press, pp. 304–26.

Brynjolfsson, E., and McAfee, A. (2014) *The Second Machine Age: Work, Progress, and Prosperity in a Time of Brilliant Technologies*. London: W. W. Norton & Company.

Bureau of Labor Statistics (1965) *Occupational Outlook Handbook, 1966–67*. US Department of Labor. http://bit.ly/2zNwLIe.

Bureau of Labor Statistics (2016, 2015, 2010, 2008, 2000) *Occupational Employment Statistics*. US Department of Labor. https://www.bls.gov/oes/tables.htm.

Burrage, M. (1997) Mrs Thatcher against the 'little republics': ideology, precedents and reactions. In T. C. Halliday and L. Karpik (eds), *Lawyers and the Rise of Western Political Liberalism*. Oxford: Clarendon Press, pp. 125–65.

Burrage, M., and Torstendahl, R. (eds) (1990) *Professions in Theory and History: Rethinking the Study of the Professions*. London: Sage.

Bush, T., Sunder, S., and Fearnley, S. (2007) *Auditor Liability Reforms in the UK and the US: A Comparative Review*. Available at SSRN: http://bit.ly/2ibC1gG.

Campbell, I., and Charlesworth, S. (2012) Salaried lawyers and billable hours: a new perspective from the sociology of work. *International Journal of the Legal Profession* 19(1): 89–122.

Campbell, R. W. (2016) *The Digital Future of the Oldest Information Profession*. Available at SSRN: http://bit.ly/2nphwCO.

Canton, E., Ciriaci, D., and Solera, I. (2014) *The Economic Impact of Professional Services Liberalisation*. European Commission, European Economy. http://bit.ly/2AqHSap.

Carr-Saunders, A. M., and Wilson, P. A. (1933) *The Professions*. Oxford: Oxford University Press.

Chafetz, M. E. (1994) *The Tyranny of Experts: Blowing the Whistle on the Cult of Expertise*. New York: Derrydale Press.

Chan, C. K., and Anteby, M. (2015) Task segregation as a mechanism for within-job inequality: Women and men of the Transportation Security Administration. *Administrative Science Quarterly* 61(2), 184–216.

Charles, M., and Grusky, D. B. (2004) *Occupational Ghettos: The Worldwide Segregation of Women and Men*. Stanford, CA: Stanford University Press.

Chreim, S., Williams, B., and Hinings, C. R. 2007. Interlevel influences on the reconstruction of professional role identity. *Academy of Management Journal* 50: 1515–39.

Christensen, C. M., Wang, D., and Von Bever, D. (2013) Consulting on the Cusp of Disruption. *Harvard Business Review* 91(October): 106–14.

Coffee, J. C. (2006) *Gatekeepers: The Professions and Corporate Governance*. Oxford: Oxford University Press.

Collins, R. (1990). Changing conceptions in the sociology of the professions. In M. Burrage and R. Torstendahl (eds), *Knowledge, State and Strategy: The Formation of Professions in Europe and North America*. London: Sage, pp. 11–23.

Cooper, D., Hinings, C. R., Greenwood, R., and Brown, J. L. (1996) Sedimentation and transformation in organizational change: the case of Canadian law firms. *Organization Studies* 17(4): 623–47.

Council of Bars and Law Societies of Europe (2015, 2010, 2008, 1999) *Lawyer Statistics*. http://bit.ly/2qcV7HA.

Cousins, C. (1987) *Controlling Social Welfare*. Brighton: Wheatsheaf.

Covaleski, M. A., Dirsmith, M. W., Heian, J. B., and Samuel, S. (1998) The calculated and the avowed: techniques of discipline and struggle over identity in big six public accounting firms. *Administrative Science Quarterly* 43(2): 293–327.

Crompton, R. (1990) Professions in the current context. *Work Employment and Society – special edition: a decade of change?* 4(5): 147–66.

Currie, G., Lockett, A., Finn, R., Martin, G. P., and Waring, J. (2012) Institutional work to maintain professional power: recreating the model of medical professionalism. *Organization Studies* 33(7), 937–62.

Currie R., Richmond J., Faulconbridge J., Gabbioneta C., and Muzio D. (2019) Professional misconduct in healthcare: setting out a research agenda for work sociology. *Work, Employment and Society* 33(1): 149–61.

Dacin, P. A., Dacin, T., and Matear, M. (2010) Social entrepreneurship: why we don't need a new theory and how we move forward from here. *Academy of Management Perspectives* 24(3): 37–57.

David, R. J., Sine, W. D., and Haveman, H. A. (2013) Seizing opportunity in emerging fields: how institutional entrepreneurs legitimated the professional form of management consulting. *Organization Science* 24(2): 356–77.

Derber, C. (ed.) (1982) *Professionals as Workers: Mental Labour in Advanced Capitalism.* Boston, MA: G. K. Hall.

Derbyshire, J. (15 November 2018) Big Four circle the legal profession. *The Financial Times.*

DeStefano, M. (2018) *Legal Upheaval: A Guide to Creativity, Collaboration, and Innovation in Law.* American Bar Association. Kindle Edition.

Dezalay, Y., and Garth, B. G. (2012) Corporate law firms, NGOs, and issues of legitimacy for a global legal order. *Fordham Law Review* 80 (6): 2309–45.

Dezalay, Y., and Garth, B. (1996) *Dealing in Virtue: International Commercial Arbitration and the Construction of a Trans-National Legal Order.* Chicago, IL: University of Chicago Press.

DiMaggio, P. J. (1991) Constructing an organizational field as a professional project: US art museums, 1920–1940. In W. W. Powell and P. J. DiMaggio (eds), *The New Institutionalism in Organizational Analysis.* Chicago, IL: University of Chicago Press, pp. 267–92.

DiMaggio, P. J., and Powell, W. (1991) Introduction. In P. J. DiMaggio and W. Powell (eds.), *The New Institutionalism in Organizational Analysis.* Chicago, IL: Chicago University Press.

DiMaggio, P. J., and Powell, W. W. (1983) The iron cage revisited: institutional isomorphism and collective rationality in organizational fields. *American Sociological Review* 48(2): 147–60.

Dinovitzer, R., Gunz, H. P., and Gunz, S. (2014) Unpacking client capture: evidence from corporate law firms. *Journal of Professions and Organization* 1(2): 99–117.

Dixon-Woods, M., Yeung, K., and Bosk, C. (2011) Why is U.K. medicine no longer a self-regulating profession? The role of scandals involving 'bad apple' doctors. *Social Science & Med.* 73(10): 1452–9.

Djelic, M.-L., and Sahlin-Andersson, K. (eds) (2006) *Transnational Governance: Institutional Dynamics of Regulation.* Cambridge: Cambridge University Press.

Durkheim, E. (1984) *The Division of Labour in Society.* New York: Macmillan Education.

Durkheim, E. (1992) *Professional Ethics and Civic Morals*, 2nd ed. London: Routledge.

Empson, L. (ed.) (2007) *Managing the Modern Law Firm: New Challenges, New Perspectives.* Oxford: Oxford University Press.

Empson, L. (2017) *Leading Professionals: Power, Politics, and Prima Donnas.* Oxford: Oxford University Press.

Empson, L., and Langley, A. (2015) Leadership and professionals: multiple manifestations of influence in professional service firms. In L. Empson, D. Muzio, J. Broschak and B. Hinings (eds), *The Oxford Handbook of Professional Service Firms.* Oxford: Oxford University Press, pp. 163–88.

Empson, L., Muzio, D., Broschak, J., and Hinings, B. (2015) Researching professional service firms: an introduction and overview. In L. Empson, D. Muzio, J. Broschack and B. Hinings (eds.), *The Oxford Handbook of Professional Services Firms.* Oxford: Oxford University Press, pp. 1–24.

Etzioni, A. (1969) *The Semi-Professions and Their Organization; Teachers, Nurses, Social Workers.* New York: Free Press.

Eyal, G. (2013) For a sociology of expertise: the social origins of the autism epidemic. *American Journal of Sociology* 118(4): 863–907.

Evetts, J. (2002) New directions in state and international professional occupations: discretionary decision-making and acquired regulation. *Work Employment and Society* 16(2): 341–52.

Evetts, J. (2011) A new professionalism? Challenges and opportunities. *Current Sociology* 59(4): 406–22.

Evetts, J. (2014) The concept of professionalism: professional work, professional practice and learning. In S., Billett, C. Harteis and H. Gruber (eds), *International Handbook of Research in Professional and Practice-Based Learning.* Ipswich: Springer, pp. 29–56.

Fama, E. F., and Jensen, M. C. (1983) Separation of ownership and control. *The Journal of Law & Economics* 26(2), 301–25.

Farndale, E., and Brewster, C. (2005) In search of legitimacy: personnel management associations worldwide. *Human Resource Management Journal* 15(3), 33–48.

Faulconbridge, J., and Muzio, D. (2008) Organizational professionalism in globalizing law firms. *Work, Employment & Society* 22(1): 7–25.

Faulconbridge, J., and Muzio, D. (2009) The financialization of large law firms: situated discourses and practices of reorganization. *Journal of Economic Geography* 9(5): 641–61.

Faulconbridge, J., and Muzio, D. (2012) Learning to be a lawyer in transnational law firms: communities of practice, institutions and identity regulation. *Global Networks* 12(1): 48–70.

Faulconbridge, J., and Muzio, D. (2015) Transnational corporations shaping institutional change: the case of English law firms in Germany. *The Journal of Economic Geography* 15(6): 1195–226.

Faulconbridge, J. and Muzio, D. (2016) Global professional service firms and the challenge of institutional complexity: 'field relocation' as a response strategy. *Journal of Management Studies* 53(1): 89–124.

Faulconbridge, J. and Muzio, D. (2019) Field partitioning: the emergence, development and consolidation of subfields. *Organizational Studies*. Forthcoming.

Fayard, A. L., Stigliani, I., & Bechky, B. A. (2017) How nascent occupations construct a mandate: the case of service designers' ethos. *Administrative Science Quarterly* 62(2): 270–303.

Ferlie, E., Fitzgerald, L., McGivern, G., Dopson, S., and Bennett, C. P. (2011) Public policy networks and 'wicked problems': a nascent solution? *Public Administration* 89(2): 307–24.

Financial & Legal Skills Partnership (2018) *Scottish Higher Level Apprenticeships: Level 4 (SCQF Level 8) A Technical Apprenticeship in Professional Services*. https://bit.ly/2YqkJRD.

Fincham, R., and Clark, T. (2002) Management consultancy: issues, perspectives, and agendas. *International Studies of Management & Organization* 32(4): 3–18.

Fligstein, N. (1990) *The Transformation of Corporate Control*. Cambridge, MA: Harvard University Press.

Flood, J. (2012) Will there be fallout from Clementi? The repercussions for the legal profession after the Legal Services Act 2007. *Michigan State Law Review*: 537–64.

Foucault, M. (1977) *Discipline and Punish*. London: Penguin.

Fournier, V. (1999) The appeal to 'professionalism' as a disciplinary mechanism. *Sociological Review* 47(2), 280–307.

Freidson, E. (1988) *Profession of Medicine: A Study of the Sociology of Applied Knowledge*. New York: Dodd, Mead and Co.

Freidson, E. (1994) *Professionalism Reborn: Theory, Prophecy and Policy*. Cambridge: Polity Press.

Freidson, E. (2001) *Professionalism: The Third Logic*. Cambridge: Polity Press.

Friedman, S., Laurison, D., and Andrew, M. (2015) Breaking the class ceiling? Social mobility into Britain's elite occupations. *The Sociological Review* 63 (2): 259–89.

Gabbioneta, C., Greenwood, R., Mazzola, P., and Minoja, M. (2013) The influence of the institutional context on corporate illegality. *Accounting, Organizations and Society* 38(6–7): 484–504.

Gabbioneta, C., Prakash, R., and Greenwood, R. (2014) Sustained corporate corruption and processes of institutional ascription within professional networks. *Journal of Professions and Organization* 1(1): 16–32.

Gabbioneta, C., Faulconbridge, J., Currie, G., Dinovitzer, R., and Muzio, D. (2018) Inserting professionals and professional organizations in studies of wrongdoing: the nature, antecedents and consequences of professional misconduct. *Human Relations*. https://doi.org/10.1177/0018726718809400.

Galambos, l. (1965) *Competition and Cooperation: The Emergence of a National Trade Association*. Baltimore: John Hopkins University Press.

Galanter, M., and Palay, T. (1991) *Tournament of Lawyers: The Transformation of the Big Law Firm*. Chicago, IL: University of Chicago Press.

Gane, M., and Johnson, T. (1993) *Foucault's New Domain*. London: Routledge

Gardner, H. K., and Eccles, R. G. (2011) Eden Mccallum: A Network-Based Consulting Firm (A) *HBS Case No. 410–056*. Available at SSRN: https://ssrn .com/abstract=1963909.

Garicano, L., and Hubbard, T. N. (2007) *The Return to Knowledge Hierarchies*. US Census Bureau Center for Economic Studies Paper No. CES-WP-07–01. Available at SSRN: http://bit.ly/2qb74NJ.

Gill, M. J. (2015) Elite identity and status anxiety: an interpretative phenomenological analysis of management consultants. *Organization* 22(3): 306–25.

Goode, W. J. (1957) Community within a community: the professions. American Sociological Review 22(2), 194–200.

Goodman J. (2016) *Robots in Law: How Artificial Intelligence Is Transforming Legal Services*. London: Arc Group. Kindle Edition.

Goodrick, E., and Reay, T. (2010). Florence Nightingale endures: legitimizing a new professional role identity. *Journal of Management Studies* 47: 55–84.

Gorman, E., and Sandefur, R. (2011) 'Golden Age', Quiescence, and Revival. *Work and Occupations* 38(3): 275–302.

Gorman, E. H. (2005) Gender Stereotypes, Same-Gender Preferences, and Organizational Variation in the Hiring of Women: Evidence from Law Firms. *American Sociological Review* 70(4): 702–28.

Gorman, E. H. (2015) Getting ahead in professional organizations: individual qualities, socioeconomic background and organizational context. *Journal of Professions and Organization* 2(2): 122–47.

Gouldner, A. W. (1957) Cosmopolitans and locals: toward an analysis of latent social roles. *Administrative Science Quarterly* 2(3): 281–306

Greenwood, R., and Empson, L. (2003) The professional partnership: relic or exemplary form of governance? *Organization Studies* 24(6): 909–33.

Greenwood, R., and Hinings, B. (1988) Organizational Design Types, Tracks and the Dynamics of Strategic Change. *Organization Studies* 9(3): 293–316.

Greenwood, R., and Hinings, B. (1993) Understanding strategic change: the contribution of archetypes. *Academy of Management Journal* 36(5): 1052–81.

Greenwood, R., and Hinings, C. R. (1996) Understanding radical organizational change: bringing together the old and new institutionalism. *Academy of Management Review* 21(4): 1022–54.

Greenwood, R., and Suddaby, R. (2006) Institutional entrepreneurship in mature fields: the Big Five accounting firms. *Academy of Management Journal* 49(1): 27–48.

Greenwood, R., Hinings, C., and Brown, J. (1990) 'P2-form' strategic management: corporate practices in professional partnerships. *Academy of Management Journal* 33(4): 725–55.

Greenwood, R., Hinings, C. R., and Brown, J. (2015) Sustainability and organizational change: an institutional perspective. In R. Henderson, R. Gulati, & M. Tushman (eds), *Leading Sustainable Change*. Oxford: Oxford University Press.

Greenwood, R., Li, S. X., Prakash, R., & Deephouse, D. L. (2005) Reputation, diversification, and organizational explanations of performance in professional service firms. *Organization Science* 16(6): 661–73.

Greenwood, R., Oliver, C., Sahlin, K., and Suddaby, R. (eds) (2008) *The SAGE Handbook of Organizational Institutionalism*. London: Sage.

Greenwood, R., Suddaby, R., and Hinings, C. R. (2002) Theorizing change: the role of professional associations in the transformation of institutionalized fields. *Academy of Management Journal* 45(1): 58–80.

Greenwood, R., Suddaby, R., and McDougald, M. (2006) Introduction. In Greenwood, R., Suddaby, R., and McDougald, M. (eds), *Professional Service Firms*. Oxford: JAI Press, 1–16.

Grey, C. (1994) Career as a project of the self and labour process discipline. *Sociology* 28(2): 479–97.

Grey, C. (2003) The real world of Enron's auditors. *Organization* 10(3): 572–6.

Gulati, M., and Scott, R. E. (2012) *The 3½ Minute Transaction: Boilerplate and the Limits of Contract Design*. Chicago: University of Chicago Press.

Gunz, H. P., and Gunz, S. P. (2006) Professional ethics in formal organizations. In R. Greenwood and R. Suddaby (eds), *Professional Service Firms – Research in the Sociology of Organizations* (Vol. 24). Cheltenham: Emerald Publishing, pp. 257–81.

Hall, R. H. (1968) Professionalization and bureaucratization, *American Sociological Review.* 33(1): 92–104.

Halliday, T. C. (1987) *Beyond Monopoly: Lawyers, State Crises, and Professional Empowerment.* Chicago, IL: University of Chicago Press.

Hanlon, G. (1998) Professionalism as enterprise: service class politics and the redefinition of professionalism. *Sociology* 32(1): 43–63.

Hansen, M. T., Nohria, N., and Tierney, T. (1999) What's your strategy for managing knowledge? *Harvard Business Review* 77(2): 106–16.

Hardy, C., and McGuire, S. (2008) Institutional entrepreneurship. In R. Greenwood, C. Oliver, R. Suddaby, and K. Sahlin (eds), *The Sage Handbook of Organizational Institutionalism.* London: Sage Publications, pp. 198–217.

Harvey, D. (2010) *The Enigma of Capital: and the Crises of Capitalism.* London: Profile Books.

Harz, M. (2017) Cancer, computers and complexity: decision making for the patient. *European Review* 25(1): 96–106.

Haug, M. (1972) Deprofessionalization: An alternative hypothesis for the future. *Sociological Review Monographs* 20(1): 195–211.

Hickson, D. J., and Thomas, M. W. (1969) Professionalization in Britain: a preliminary measure. *Sociology* 3(1): 37–53.

Hinings, C. R. (2005). The changing nature of professional organizations. In S. Ackroyd, R. Batt, P. Thompson, and P. S. Tolbert (eds), *The Oxford Handbook of Work and Organization.* Oxford: Oxford University Press, pp. 404–24.

Hodgson, D. E., Paton, S., and Muzio, D. (2015) Something old, something new? Competing logics and the hybrid nature of new corporate professions. *British Journal of Management* 26(4): 745–59.

Hoffman, A. (1999) Institutional evolution and change: environmentalism and the US chemical industry. *Academy of Management Journal* 42(4): 351–71.

Hudson, J. R. (2013) *Special Interest Society.* New York: Lexington Books.

Hughes, E. C. (1963) Profession. *Daedalus* 92(4): 55–68.

Huising, R. (2015) To hive or to hold? Producing professional authority through scut work. *Administrative Science Quarterly* 60(2): 263–99.

Hwang, H., and Powell, W. W. (2009) The rationalisation of charity: the influences of professionalism in the non-profit sector. *Administrative Science Quarterly* 54(2): 268–98.

Ibarra, H. (1999) Provisional selves: experimenting with image and identity in professional adaptation. *Administrative Science Quarterly* 44: 764–91.

Illich, I. (1976) *Medical Nemesis: The Expropriation of Health*. New York: Pantheon Books.

Illich, I. (1977) *Disabling Professions*. New York: Marion Boyars.

Insights West (15 June 2017) Nurses, Doctors and Scientists Are Canada's Most Respected Professionals. http://bit.ly/2Fys3Uf.

Ipsos MORI (2017) *Trust in Professions: Long-Term Trends*. http://bit.ly /2G97xan.

Iyer, V. M., Bamber, E. M., and Barefield, R. M. (2000) CPA firms' marketing strategies: the important role of alumni relations programs. *Journal of Professional Services Marketing* 21(1): 1–7.

Jenkins, K. (2017) *Exploring the UK Freelance Workforce in 2016*. London: IPSE.

Ježek, P., and Jeppe, K. (2017) *Report on the inquiry into money laundering, tax avoidance and tax evasion*. European Parliament. http://bit.ly/2HyndU0.

Johnson, T. J. (1972) *Professions and Power*. London: Macmillan

Johnson, T. L. (1977) Professions in the class structure. In R. Scase (ed.), *Class, Cleavage and Control*. London: Allen and Unwin, pp. 93–110.

Johnson, T. L. (1982) The state and the professions: peculiarities of the British. In A. Giddens and G. Mackenzie (eds), *Social Class and the Division of Labour*. Cambridge: Cambridge University Press, pp. 186–208.

Kaplan, J. (2015) *Humans Need Not Apply: A Guide to Wealth and Work in the Age of Artificial Intelligence*: New Haven, CT: Yale University Press.

Kay, F. M., Alarie, S., and Adjei, J. (2013) Leaving private practice: how organizational context, time pressures, and structural inflexibilities shape departures from private law practice. *Indiana Journal of Global Legal Studies* 20(2), 1223–60.

Kershaw, D., and Moorhead, R. (2013) Consequential responsibility for client wrongs: Lehman Brothers and the regulation of the legal profession. *The Modern Law Review* 76(1): 26–61.

Keystone Law (11 May 2015) *Law firm's installation at Liverpool Street Station tells commuters legal careers don't have to be this way*. http://bit.ly /2CpnmKt.

Khosla, V. (4 December 2012) Technology will replace 80% of what doctors do. *Fortune*. http://for.tn/2rL4XAp.

Kipping, M. (2002). Trapped in their wave: the evolution of management consultancies. In T. Clark and R. Fincham (eds), *Critical Consulting: New Perspectives on the Management Advice Industry*. Oxford: Blackwell, pp. 28–49.

Kipping, M. (2011) Hollow from the start? Image professionalism in management consulting. *Current Sociology* 59(4): 530–50.

Kipping, M., and Kirkpatrick, I. (2013) Alternative pathways of change in professional services firms: the case of management consulting. *Journal of Management Studies* 50(5): 777–807.

Kipping, M., Kirkpatrick, I., and Muzio, D. (2006) Overly controlled or out of control? Management consultants and the new corporate professionalism. In J. Craig (ed.), *Production Values: Futures for Professionalism*. London: Demos, pp. 153–65.

Kirkpatrick, I., and Ackroyd, S. (2003) Archetype theory and the changing professional organization: a critique and alternative. *Organization* 10(4): 739–58.

Kirkpatrick, I., and Hoque, K. (2006) A retreat from permanent employment? Accounting for the rise of professional agency work in UK public services. *Work, Employment and Society* 20(4): 649–66.

Kirkpatrick, I., Muzio, D., and Aulakh, S. (2017) *Practice-to-Profession: Exploration of the Current Status, Perceptions and Future Pathways*. Chicago, IL: ASAE Foundation.

Kirkpatrick, I., Muzio, D., Kipping, M., and Hinnings, C. R. (2019) Meta organisations and the emergence of corporate professionalism: the case of UK management consulting'. Paper presented at the American Academy of Management conference, Boston, August.

Kleiner, M. M., and Krueger, A. B. (2013) Analyzing the extent and influence of occupational licensing on the labor market. *Journal of Labor Economics* 31 (2), S173–S202.

Kleiner, M. M., and Vorotnikov, E. (2017) Analyzing occupational licensing among the states. *Journal of Regulatory Economics* 52(2): 132–58.

Kleiner, M. M. (2013) *Stages of Occupational Regulation*. Kalamazoo, MI: Upjohn Institute for Employment Research.

Kmec, J., and Gorman, E. H. (2009) Gender and discretionary work effort: evidence from the United States and Britain. *Work and Occupations* 37(1): 3–36.

Kornberger, M., Carter, C., and Ross-Smith, A. (2010) Changing gender domination in a Big Four accounting firm: Flexibility, performance and client service in practice. *Accounting, Organizations and Society* 35(8): 775–91.

Kornberger, M., Justesen, L., and Mouritsen, J. (2011) 'When you make manager, we put a big mountain in front of you': an ethnography of managers in a Big 4 accounting firm. *Accounting, Organizations and Society* 36(8): 514–33.

Koumenta, M., and Pagliero, M. (2017) *Measuring Prevalence and Labour Market Impacts of Occupational Regulation in the EU*. European Commission. http://bit.ly/2qeTj0C.

Krause, E. A. (1996) *The Death of the Guilds: Professions, States and the Advance of Capitalism*. New Haven, CT: Yale University Press.

Krill, P. R., Johnson, R., and Albert, L. (2016) The prevalence of substance use and other mental health concerns among American attorneys. *Journal of Addiction Medicine* 10(1): 46–52.

Kuhlmann, E., Burau, V., Correia, T., Lewandowski, R., Lionis, C., Noordegraff, M., and Repullo, J. (2013) A manager in the minds of doctors: a comparison of new modes of control in European hospitals. *BMC Health Services Research* 13(1): 246–57.

Kuruvilla, S., and Noronha, E. (2015) From pyramids to diamonds: legal process offshoring, employment systems, and labor markets for lawyers in the United States and India. *Industrial and Labor Relations Review* 69(2): 1–24.

Kyratsis, Y., Atun, R., Phillips, N., Tracey, P., and George, G. (2017) Health systems in transition: professional identity work in the context of shifting institutional logics. *Academy of Management Journal* 60(2): 610–41.

Larson, M. S. (1977) *The Rise of Professionalism: A Sociological Analysis*. Berkeley: University of California Press.

Law, M. T. and Kim, S. (2005) Specialisation and regulation: the rise of professionals and the emergence of occupational licensing regulation. *The Journal of Economic History* 65(3): 723–56.

Lawrence, T. B. and Suddaby, R. (2006) Institutions and institutional work. In S. R. Clegg, C. Hardy, T. B. Lawrence and W. R. Nord (eds), *Handbook of Organizations Studies*, 2nd ed. London: Sage, pp. 215–54.

Leblebici, H., and Sherer, P. D. (2015) Governance in professional service firms: from structural and cultural to legal normative views. In L. Empson, D. Muzio, J. Broschak and B. Hinings (eds), *The Oxford Handbook of Professional Service Firms*. Oxford: Oxford University Press, pp. 189–212.

Leicht, K. T. (2016) Market fundamentalism, cultural fragmentation, post-modern scepticism, and the future or professional work. *Journal of Professions and Organization* 3(1): 103–17.

Leicht, K. T., and Fennell, M. (2001) *Professional Work: A Sociological Approach*. Oxford: Blackwell.

Leicht, K. T., and Fennell, M. L. (1997) The changing organizational context of professional work. *Annual Review of Sociology* 23: 215–31.

Leicht, K. T., and Lyman, E. C. (2006) Markets, institutions, and the crisis of professional practice. In R. Greenwood and R. Suddaby (eds), *Research in the Sociology of Organizations* (Vol. 4). Cheltenham: Emerald Publishing, pp. 17–44.

Lepisto, D. A., Crosina, E., and Pratt, M. G. (2015) Identity work within and beyond the professions: toward a theoretical integration and extension. In A. Desilva and M. Aparicio (eds), *International Handbook of Professional Identities*. Rosemead, CA: Scientific and Academic Publishing, pp. 11–37.

Lester, S. (2009) Routes to qualified status: practices and trends among UK professional bodies. *Studies in Higher Education* 34(2): 223–36.

Lester, S. (2016) The development of self-regulation in four UK professional communities. *Professions and Professionalism* 6(1): 1441. https://journals.hioa.no/index.php/pp/article/view/1441

Lieberman, J. (1970) *The Tyranny of the Experts*: New York: Basic Books.

Lounsbury, M. (2001) Institutional sources of practice variation: staffing college and university recycling programs. *Administrative Science Quarterly* 46(1): 29–56.

Lounsbury, M. (2002) Institutional transformation and status mobility: the professionalization of the field of finance. *Academy of Management Journal* 45(1): 255–66.

Lounsbury, M. (2007) A tale of two cities: competing logics and practice variation in the professionalization of mutual funds. *Academy of Management Journal* 50(2): 289–307.

Lounsbury, M., and Kaghan, B. (2001) Organizations, occupations and the structuration of work. In S. P. Vallas (ed.),*The Transformation of Work (Research in the Sociology of Work)* (Vol. 10). Cheltenham: Emerald Group Publishing, pp. 25–50.

Lupu, I., and Empson, L. (2015) Illusio and overwork: playing the game in the accounting field. *Accounting, Auditing and Accountability Journal* 28(8): 1310–40.

Lyons, B. D., Mueller, L. M., Gruys, M. L. and Meyers, A. J. (2012) A re-examination of the web-based job demand for PHR and SPHR certifications in the United States. *Human Resource Management* 51(5): 769–88.

MacDonald, K. M. (1995) *The Sociology of the Professions*. London: Sage.

Maister, D. (2003) *Managing the Professional Service Firm*. New York: Simon Schuster.

Malhotra, N., and Hinings, C. R. (2010) An organizational model for understanding internationalization processes. *Journal of International Business Studies* 41(2): 330–49.

Malhotra, N., Morris, T., and Smets, M. (2010) New career models in UK professional service firms: from up-or-out to up-and-going-nowhere? *The International Journal of Human Resource Management* 21(9): 1396–1413.

Malhotra, N., Morris, T., and Hinings, C. B. (2006) Variation in organizational form among professional service organizations. In R. Greenwood and R. Suddaby (eds), *Professional Service Firms: Research in the Sociology of*

Organizations (Vol. 24). Cheltenham: Emerald Group Publishing, pp. 171–202.

Malhotra, N., Smets, M., and Morris, T. (2016) Career pathing and innovation in professional service firms. *Academy of Management Perspectives* 30(4): 369–83.

Malos, S. B., and Champion, M. A. (2000). Human resource strategy and career mobility in professional service firms: a test of an options-based model. *Academy of Management Journal* 43(4): 749–60.

Marshall, T. H. (1939) The recent history of professionalism in relation to social structure and social policy. *The Canadian Journal of Economics and Political Science* 5(3): 325–40.

Martin, G. P., Kocman, D., Stephens, T., Peden, C. J., and Pearse, R. M. (2017) Pathways to professionalism? Quality improvement, care pathways, and the interplay of standardisation and clinical autonomy. *Sociology of Health and Illness* 39(8): 1–16.

Mawdsley, J. K., and Somaya, D. (2015) Strategy and strategic alignment in professional service firms. In L. Empson, D. Muzio, J. Broschak and B. Hinings (eds), *The Oxford Handbook of Professional Service Firms*. Oxford: Oxford University Press, pp. 213–37.

Mawdsley, J. K. and Somaya, D. (2018) Demand-side strategy, relational advantage, and partner-driven corporate scope: The case for client-led diversification. *Strategic Management Journal* 39(7): 1834–59.

Mazmanian, M., Orlikowski, W. J., and Yates, J. (2013) The autonomy paradox: the implications of mobile e-mail devices for knowledge professionals. *Organization Science* 27(5): 1337–57.

McCarthy, N. (4 January 2018) America's most and least trusted professions. *Forbes*. http://bit.ly/2Hfd1zN.

McClelland, C. E. (1991) *The German Experience of Professionalization*. Cambridge: Cambridge University Press.

McGinnis, J. O., and Pearce, R. G. (2014) The great disruption: how machine intelligence will transform the role of lawyers in the delivery of legal services. *Fordham Law Review* 82(6): 3041–66.

McKenna, C. D. (2006) *The World's Newest Profession: Management Consultancy in the Twentieth Century*. New York: Cambridge University Press.

Merton, R. K. (1982) Institutionalized altruism: the case of the professions. In R. K. Merton (ed.), *Social Research and the Practicing Professions*. Cambridge, MA: ABT Books, pp. 109–34.

Meyer, J. W., and Rowan, B. (1977) Institutionalized organizations: formal structure as myth and ceremony. *American Journal of Sociology* 82(2), 340–63.

Micelotta, E. R., and Washington, M. (2013) Institutions and maintenance: the repair work of Italian professions. *Organization Studies* 34(8): 1137–70.

Millerson, G. (1964) *The Qualifying Associations: A Study in Professionalization*. London: Routledge and Kegan Paul.

Mintzberg, H. (1979) *The Structuring of Organizations: A Synthesis of the Research*. Irving, TX: Pearson.

Mitchell, A., and Sikka, P. (2011) *The Pin-Stripe Mafia: How Accountancy Firms Destroy Societies*. Basildon: Association for Accountancy and Business Affairs.

Morgan, G., and Quack, S. (2006) The Internationalisation of Professional Service Firms: Global Convergence, National Path-Dependency or Cross-Border Hybridisation? In R. Greenwood and R. Suddaby (eds), *Professional Service Firms: Research in the Sociology of Organizations*. Cheltenham: Emerald Publishing, pp. 403–31.

Morgan, R. (2017) *Health professionals continue domination with Nurses most highly regarded again; followed by Doctors and Pharmacists*. Roy Morgan Professions Survey. http://bit.ly/2HidVLY.

Morris, T. J., and Pinnington, A. H. (1998) Evaluating strategic fit in professional service firms. *Human Resource Management Journal* 8(4): 76–87.

Muhr, S. L. (2011) Caught in the gendered machine: on the masculine and feminine in cyborg leadership. *Gender, Work and Organization* 18(3): 337–57.

Murphy, R. (1986) Weberian closure theory: a contribution to the ongoing assessment. *British Journal of Sociology* 37(1): 21–41.

Muzio, D., and Ackroyd, S. (2005) On the consequences of defensive professionalism: the transformation of the legal labour process. *Journal of Law and Society* 32(4): 615–42.

Muzio, D., and Faulconbridge, J. (2013) The global professional service firm: 'one firm' models versus (Italian) distant institutionalized practices. *Organization Studies* 34(7): 897–925.

Muzio, D., and Kirkpatrick, I. (2011) Introduction: professions and organizations – a conceptual framework. *Current Sociology* 59(4): 389–405.

Muzio, D., Brock, D. M., and Suddaby, R. (2013) Professions and institutional change: towards an institutionalist sociology of the professions. *Journal of Management Studies* 50(5): 699–721.

Muzio, D., Faulconbridge, J., Gabbioneta, C., and Greenwood, R. (2016) Bad apples, bad barrels and bad cellars: a 'boundaries' perspective on professional misconduct. In D. Palmer, R. Greenwood and K. Smith-Crowe (eds), *Organizational Wrongdoing*. Cambridge: Cambridge University Press, pp. 141–75.

Nichols, T. (2017) *The Death of Expertise.* New York: Oxford University Press.

Noonan, M. C., and Corcoran, M. E. (2004) The mommy track and partnership: temporary delay or dead end? *The ANNALS of the American Academy of Political and Social Science* 596(1): 130–50.

Noordegraaf, M. (2011) Risky business: how professionals and professionals fields (must) deal with organizational issues. *Organization Studies* 32(10): 1349–71.

O'Mahoney, J., and Sturdy, A. (2016) Power and the diffusion of management ideas: the case of McKinsey & Co. *Management Learning* 47(3): 247–65.

OECD (2007) *Competitive Restrictions in Legal Professions.* http://bit.ly /2jafjqk.

OECD Health Statistics (2017) http://bit.ly/2qp6g7W.

Office for National Statistics (2017a) *UK business; activity, size and location: Statistical Bulletin.* http://bit.ly/2GwJpPg.

Office for National Statistics (2017b) *Input-output supply and use tables: summary tables.* http://bit.ly/2GuXv3y.

Oppenheimer, M. (1972) The proletarianization of the professional. *The Sociological Review* 20(51): 213–27.

Oppenheimer, M. (1973) Proletarianization of the professional. In P. Halmos (ed.), *Professionalization and Social Change.* Keele: Keele University Press, 213–27.

Park, S., Sine, W. D., and Tolbert, P. S. (2011). Professions, organizations, and institutions: tenure systems in colleges and universities. *Work and Occupations* 38(3): 340–71.

Parker, C. (2008) Peering over the ethical precipice: incorporation, listing and the ethical responsibilities of law firms. Available at SSRN: http://bit.ly /2jEl7Yo

Parkin, F. (1974) Strategies of social closure in class formation. In F. Parkin (ed.), *The Social Analysis of Class Structure.* London: Tavistock Publications, pp. 1–18.

Parks-Leduc, L., Rutherford, M., Becker, K., and Shahzad, A. (2017) The professionalization of human resource management: examining undergraduate curricula and the influence of professional organizations. *Journal of Management Education* 42(2): 211–38.

Parsons, T. (1954) Professional and social structure. In T. Parsons (ed.), *Essays in Sociological Theory.* Glencoe: Free Press, pp. 34–49.

Paton, P. D. (2010) Multidisciplinary Practice Redux: Globalization, Core Values, and Reviving the MDP Debate in America. *Fordham Law Review* 78(5): 2193–244.

Pelkmans, J. (2017) *The New Restrictiveness Indicator for Professional Services: An Assessment.* European Commission.

Peteraf, M. A. (1993) The cornerstones of competitive advantage: a resource-based view. *Strategic Management Journal* 14(3): 171–91.

Philipsen, N. J. (2009) Regulation of liberal professions and competition policy: developments in the EU and China. *Journal of Competition Law and Economics* 6(2): 203–31.

Pichault, P., and McKeown, T. (2019) Autonomy at work in the gig economy: analysing work status, work content and working conditions of independent professionals. *New Technology, Work and Employment* 34(1): 59–72.

Population Reference Bureau (2016, 2010, 2001) *World Population Data Sheets*. http://bit.ly/2zJNpdK.

Powell, M. J., Brock, D. M., and Hinings, C. R. (1999) The changing professional organization. In M. J. Powell, D. M. Brock, and C. R. Hinings (eds), *Restructuring the Professional Organization: Accounting, Health Care, and Law*. London: Routledge, pp. 1–19.

Professional Associations Research Network (PARN) (2015) *Professional Body Sector Review 2015*. Bristol: PARN Global.

Quack, S., and Schüßler, E. (2015) Dynamics of regulation of professional service firms: national and transnational developments. In L. Empson, D. Muzio, J. Broschack and B. Hinings (eds), *The Oxford Handbook of Professional Services Firms*. Oxford: Oxford University Press, pp. 48–70.

Raelin, J. A. (1991) *The Clash of Cultures: Managers Managing Professionals*. Boston: Harvard Business School Press.

Reader, W. J. (1966) *Professional Men: The Rise of the Professional Classes in Nineteenth Century England*. London: Weidenfeld and Nicolson.

Redbird, B. (2017) The new closed shop? The economic and structural effects of occupational licensure. *American Sociological Review* 82(3): 600–24.

Reed, M. (1996) Expert power and control in late modernity: an empirical review and theoretical synthesis. *Organization Studies* 17(4): 573–97.

Reed, M. (2007) Engineers of human souls, faceless technocrats or merchants of morality? Changing professional forms and identities in the face of the neoliberal challenge. In A. Pinnington, R. Macklin, and T. Campbell (eds), *Human Resource Management: Ethics and Employment*. Oxford: Oxford University Press, pp. 171–89.

Rego, R., and Vardana, M. (2009) Professional associations. In H. K. Anheier and R. Toepler (eds), *International Encyclopaedia of Civil Society*. Springer Press, pp. 1250–5.

Remus, D., and Levey, F. (2016) *Can Robots Be Lawyers? Computers, Lawyers, And The Practice Of Law.* Available at SSRN: http://bit.ly/2Ao2nGW.

Rhode, D. L. (2015) *The Trouble with Lawyers.* Oxford: Oxford University Press.

Ritzer, G., and Walczak, D. (1986) The changing nature of American medicine. *The Journal of American Culture* 9(4): 43–51.

Rose, T., and Hinings, C. R. (1999) Global clients' demands driving change in global business advisory firms. In D. M. Brock, C. R. Hinings, and M. J. Powell (eds), *Restructuring the Professional Organization.* London: Routledge, pp. 41–67.

Sako, M. 2015 Outsourcing and offshoring of professional services. In L. Empson, D. Muzio, J. Broschak and B. Hinings (eds), *The Handbook of Professional Services Firms.* Oxford: Oxford University Press, pp. 327–47.

Saks, M. (2015) *The Professions, State and the Market: Medicine in Britain, the United States and Russia.* Abingdon: Routledge.

Saks, M. (2016) Professions and power: a review of theories of professions and power. In M. Dent, I. L. Bourgeault, J. Denis, and E. Kuhlmann (eds), *The Routledge Companion to the Professions and Professionalism.* London: Routledge, pp. 71–86.

Samsonova-Taddei, A., and Humphrey, C. (2014) Transnationalism and the transforming roles of professional accountancy bodies: towards a research agenda. *Accounting, Auditing & Accountability Journal* 27(6): 903–32.

Sandholtz, K., Chung, D., and Waisberg, I. (2019) The double-edged sword of jurisdictional entrenchment: explaining human resources professionals' failed strategic repositioning. *Organization Science.* https://doi.org/10.1287/orsc.2019.1282.

Schneyer, T. (2013) 'Professionalism' as pathology: the ABA's latest policy debate on non-lawyer ownership of law practice entities. *Fordham Urban Law Journal* 40(1): 75–138.

Schön, D. (1983). *The Reflective Practitioner.* New York: Basic Books.

Schwab, K. (2016) *The Fourth Industrial Revolution.* London: Penguin.

Sciulli, D. (2005) Continental sociology of professions today: Conceptual contributions. *Current Sociology* 53(6): 915–42.

Scott, C. (1966) Professionals in bureaucracies – areas of conflict. In H. M. Vollmer and D. L. Mills (eds), *Professionalization.* Upper Saddle River, NJ: Prentice-Hall, pp. 265–75.

Scott, W. R. (1965) Reactions to supervision in a heteronomous professional organization. *Administrative Science Quarterly* 10(1): 65–81.

Scott, W. R. (2008) Lords of the dance: professionals as institutional agents. *Organizational Studies* 29(2): 219–38.

Scott, W. R., Ruef, M., Mendel, P. J., and Caronna, C. A. (2000) *Institutional Change and Healthcare Organizations*. Chicago, IL: University of Chicago Press.

Sharma, A. (1997) Professional as agent: knowledge asymmetry in agency exchange. *Academy of Management Review* 22(3): 758–98.

Siebert, S., Martin, G., and Bozic, B. (2016) Research into employee trust: epistemological foundations and paradigmatic boundaries. *Human Resource Management Journal* 26(3): 269–84.

Siggelkow, N. (2002) Evolution toward Fit. *Administrative Science Quarterly* 47(1): 125–59.

Sikka, P. (2015) No accounting for tax avoidance. *The Political Quarterly* 86 (3): 427–33.

Sikka, P., and Willmott, H. (2011) The dark side of transfer pricing: its role in tax avoidance and wealth retentiveness. *Critical Perspectives on Accounting* 21(4): 342–56.

Sikka, P., and Willmott, H. (2013) The tax avoidance industry: accountancy firms on the make. *Critical Perspectives on International Business* 9(4): 415–43.

Sikka, P., and Willmott, H. (2018) Regulating money laundering: a case study of the UK experience. In G. Morgan and L. Engwall (eds), *Regulation and Organizations: International Perspectives: Volume 28. Industrial Economics*. Kindle Edition. Abingdon: Routledge, pp. 248–70.

Smets, M., Morris, T., and Malhotra, N. (2011) Changing career models and capacity for innovation in professional services. In M. Reihlen and A. Werr (eds), *Handbook of Research on Entrepreneurship in Professional Service Firms*. Cheltenham: Edward Elgar, pp. 127–47.

Smets, M., Morris, T., Von Nordenflycht, A., and Brock, D. M. (2017) 25 years since 'P2': Taking stock and charting the future of professional firms. *Journal of Professions and Organization* 4(2): 91–111.

Sommerlad, H., and Ashley, L. (2015) Diversity and inclusion. In L. Empson, D. Muzio, and J. Broschak (eds), *The Oxford Handbook of Professional Service Firms*. Oxford: Oxford University Press, pp. 452–75.

Spillman, L. (2012) *Solidarity in Strategy*. London: University of Chicago Press.

Spillman, L. (2018) Meta-organization matter. *Journal of Management Inquiry* 27(1): 16–20.

Spillman, L., and Brophy, S. A. (2018) Professionalism as a cultural form: knowledge, craft, and moral agency. *Journal of Professions and Organization* 5(2), 155–66.

Stephen, F. H. (2013) *Lawyers, Markets and Regulation*. Cheltenham: Edward Elgar.

Stiglitz, J. (2013) *The Price of Inequality*. London: Penguin.

Suddaby, R., and Greenwood, R. (2001) Colonizing knowledge: commodification as a dynamic of jurisdictional expansion in professional service firms.
Human Relations 54(7): 933–53.

Suddaby, R., and Muzio, D. (2015) Theoretical perspective on the professions.
In L. Empson, D. Muzio, J. Broschack and B. Hinings (eds), *The Oxford
Handbook of Professional Services Firms*. Oxford: Oxford University Press,
pp. 25–47.

Suddaby, R., and Viale, T. (2011) Professionals and field-level change:
Institutional work and the professional project. *Current Sociology* 59(4):
423–41.

Suddaby, R., Cooper, D. J., and Greenwood, R. (2007) Transnational regulation
of professional services: governance dynamics of field level organizational
change. *Accounting Organizations and Society* 32(4–5): 333–62.

Susskind, R., and Susskind, D. (2015) *The Future of the Professions: How
Technology Will Transform the Work of Human Experts*. Oxford: Oxford
University Press.

Švarc, J. (2016) The knowledge worker is dead: what about professions?
Current Sociology 64(3): 392–410.

Terry, L. (2009) The European Commission project regarding competition in
professional services. *Northwestern Journal of International Law and
Business* 29(1): 1–117.

The Law Society (2016) *Trends in the Solicitors' Profession: Annual Statistical
Review*. London: The Law Society.

The Law Society (2019) *Lawtech Adoption Research*. London: The Law
Society. http://bit.ly/2FBA7kX.

Thomson Reuters, Oxford Saïd Business School and the Georgetown Law
Center for the Study of the Legal Profession. (2017) *Alternative legal service
providers: Understanding the growth and benefits of these new legal providers*. http://tmsnrt.rs/2B0bGtH.

Thornton, M. (2016) Squeezing the life out of lawyers: legal practice in the
market embrace. *Griffith Law Review* 25(4): 471–91.

Thornton, P. H. (2002) The rise of the corporation in a craft industry: conflict and
conformity in institutional logics. *Academy of Management Journal* 45: 81–101.

Thornton, P. H., and Ocasio, W. (1999) Institutional logics and the historical
contingency of power in organizations: executive succession in the higher
education publishing industry, 1958–1990. *American Journal of Sociology*
105(3): 801–43.

Thornton, P. H., Ocasio, W., and Lounsbury, M. (2012). *The Institutional Logics
Perspective*. Oxford: Oxford University Press.

Thornton, R. J., and Timmons, E. J. (2015) The de-licensing of occupations in the United States. *Monthly Labor Review.* http://bit.ly/2q9960V.

Timmermans, S. (2008) Professions and their work: do market shelters protect professional interests? *Work and Occupations* 35(2): 164–88.

Timmons, S. (2010) Professionalization and its discontents, *Health* 15(4): 337–52.

Tolbert, P. (1996) Occupations, organizations, and boundary-less careers. In M. D. Arthur and D. M. Rousseau (eds), *The Boundary-less Career.* New York: Oxford University Press, pp. 331–49.

Tomlinson, J., Baird, M., Berg, P., and Cooper, R. (2018). Flexible careers across the life course: advancing theory, research and practice. *Human Relations* 71(1): 4–22.

Tomlinson, J., Muzio, D., Sommerlad, H., Webley, L., and Duff, L. (2013) Structure, agency and the career strategies of white women and BME individuals in the legal profession. *Human Relations* 66(2): 245–69.

Topol, E. (2015) *The Patient Will See You Now: The Future of Medicine is in Your Hands.* New York: Basic Books.

Torstendahl, R. (1990) Introduction: promotion and strategies of knowledge-based groups. In R. Torstendahl and M. Burrage (eds), *The Formation of the Professions.* London: Sage, pp. 1–10.

Townley, B. (1994) *Reframing Human Resource Management: Power, Ethics and the Subject at Work.* London: Sage.

Trautman, L. J. (2017) Following the money: lessons from the Panama Papers: part 1: tip of the iceberg. *Penn State Law Review* 121: 807–73. Available at SSRN: https://ssrn.com/abstract=2783503.

Tschirhart, M., Lee, C., and Travinin, G. (2011) *The Benefits of Credentialising Programmes to Membership Organizations.* Washington: ASAE Foundation.

Vaheesan, S., and Pasquale, P. (2018) The politics of professionalism: reappraising occupational licensure and competition policy, *Annual Review of Law and Social Science* 14: 309–27.

Van Maanen, J., and Barley, S. (1984) Occupational communities: culture and control in organizations. *Research in Organizational Behaviour* 6: 287–365.

Van Wijk, J. V., Stam, W., Elfring, T., Zietsma, C., and Den Hond, F. (2013) Activists and incumbents structuring change: the interplay of agency, culture and networks in field evolution. *Academy of Management Journal* 56(2): 358–86.

Verbeeten, F. H. M., and Speklé, R. F. (2015) Management control, results-oriented culture and public sector performance: empirical evidence on new public management. *Organization Studies* 36(7): 953–78.

Von Nordenflycht, A. (2010) What is a professional service firm? Toward a theory and taxonomy of knowledge intensive firms. *Academy of Management Review* 35(1): 155–74.

Von Nordenflycht, A. (2014) Does the emergence of publicly traded professional service firms undermine the theory of the professional partnership? A cross-industry historical analysis. *Journal of Professions and Organization* 1 (2): 137–60.

Wajcman, J. (2017) Automation: is it really different this time? *The British Journal of Sociology* 68(1): 119–27.

Weeden, K. A. (2002) Why do some occupations pay more than others? Social closure and earnings inequality in the United States. *American Journal of Sociology* 108(1): 55–101.

Weeden, K. A., and Grusky, D. B. (2014) Inequality and market failure. *American Behavioral Scientist* 58(3): 473–91.

Wilensky, H. L. (1964) The professionalization of everyone? *American Journal of Sociology* 70(2): 137–58.

Wilkins, D. B., and Gulati, G. M. (1996) Why are there so few black lawyers in corporate law firms? An institutional analysis. *California Law Review* 84(3): 496–625.

Wilkins, D. B., and Gulati, G. M. (1998) Reconceiving the tournament of lawyers: tracking seeding and information control in internal labour markets. *Virginia Law Review* 84(4): 1581–681.

Williams, M., and Koumenta, M. (2019) Occupational closure and job quality: The case of occupational licensing in Britain. *Human Relations*: 1–26 (online ready).

Witz, A. (1991) *Professions and Patriarchy*. London: Routledge.

Wright, A. L., Zammuto, R. F., and Liesch, P. W. (2017) Maintaining the values of a profession: institutional work and moral emotions in the emergency department. *Academy of Management Journal* 60(1): 200–37.

Young, S. D. (2002) *The Concise Encyclopaedia of Economics: Occupational Licensing*. http://bit.ly/2qbE5JI.

Zuboff, S. (1988) *In the Age of the Smart Machine: The Future of Work and Power*. New York: Basic Books.

Acknowledgements

We would like to thank the ASAE Foundation for commissioning us to explore professionalization processes in the modern era. Of course, the financial support was very welcome, but the interest in professionalization and professional organizations that this subsequently sparked is to us of even greater value, not least because it provided the impetus for this text. Much of the foundational material in section 4 of this work is drawn from our ASAE study.

Daniel Muzio would also like to thank Helena Serra, Teresa Carvalho and the other organizer and delegates of the 2013 Apisot conference where some of these ideas were initially presented.

Cambridge Elements ☰

Organization Theory

Nelson Phillips
Imperial College London
Nelson Phillips is the Abu Dhabi Chamber Professor of Strategy and Innovation at Imperial College London. His research interests include organization theory, technology strategy, innovation, and entrepreneurship, often studied from an institutional theory perspective.

Royston Greenwood
University of Alberta
Royston Greenwood is the Telus Professor of Strategic Management at the University of Alberta, a Visiting Professor at the University of Cambridge, and a Visiting Professor at the University of Edinburgh. His research interests include organizational change and professional misconduct.

About the Series
Organization theory covers many different approaches to understanding organizations. Its focus is on what constitutes the how and why of organizations and organizing, bringing understanding of organizations in a holistic way. The purpose of *Elements in Organization Theory* is to systematize and contribute to our understanding of organizations.

Cambridge Elements $\equiv$

Organization Theory